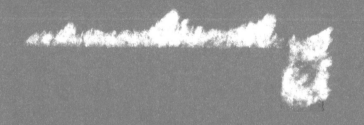

# BE MY BABY

# BE MY BABY

Parents and Children Talk About Adoption

Gail Kinn

Photographs by Ken Shung

Artisan ~ New York

Published by Artisan
A Division of Workman Publishing Company, Inc.
708 Broadway
New York, New York 10003
www.workman.com

Library of Congress Cataloging-in-Publication Data
Kinn, Gail.
Be my baby : parents and children talk about adoption / Gail Kinn ; photographs by Ken Shung.
p. cm.
ISBN 1-57965-152-6
1. Adoption—United States—Case studies.   2. Adoptive parents—United States—Case
studies.   3. Adoptees—United States—Case Studies.   I. Title.
HV875.55.K53 2000
362.73'4'0973—dc21          99-056972

Printed in Hong Kong

10 9 8 7 6 5 4 3 2 1

*Book design by Dania Davey*

This book is dedicated to Sarah Kinn,
who loves to ride horses, to read books, and
the taste of Dulce de Leche ice cream.

May your life be filled with many loves.

# Contents

# Introduction

One night, ten years ago, my brother and his wife called me from a hotel in a small town: "We have our baby girl," my brother said, "and she's so beautiful." They had learned only the day before about the birth of the daughter they were about to adopt. After picking up a car seat and a few pieces of clothing, they rushed to catch a plane to pick her up and bring her home. They had waited so long for her arrival, and now they barely had an extra diaper. "Where is she going to sleep?" I asked. "We tried the drawer, but she cried," they answered.

Sarah was my brother's first child, and our family's joy in her was immeasurable. We were transfixed by her; we sketched her luminous face as she lay sleeping, and danced around the room with her when she was awake. But we had numerous questions, too, about what being an adopted family would mean.

Raising a family, any family, demands what is best in us and often brings out what is worst. It requires us to understand what we sometimes don't, tries our patience, and rewards us with an unparalleled kind of love. Would an adoptive family be even more demanding? How difficult would it be to answer Sarah's questions about being adopted? Would even the smallest problem be seen as an "adoption problem"? We wondered, too, about how Sarah would feel about being adopted. Would she feel a sense of loss? Would she know deep in her heart that we were her family? And how might her thoughts and feelings change throughout her life?

These questions weighed on me, as well as on her parents, not only because they are valid questions, but because my brother's and my own childhood resonated some with Sarah's adoption. As the children of parents who grew up in rural central European villages and survived the Holocaust, my brother and I had had to integrate our parents' vastly different lives, and their dramatic, bewildering history, into who we were in our normal, modern life in America. Both of us wondered if Sarah, as an adopted child, would face similar challenges integrating her bewilderment about her origins and the different way she came to her family into a solid sense of who she was. For myself, the only way to address all of our questions, I decided, would be to listen to the stories of other adoptive families.

Once I began talking to people, almost everyone revealed some personal experience with adoption; a recent study states that six in ten Americans have such a connection. Whether they themselves, a family member, or close friend have adopted, or were considering doing so, adoption was clearly more a part of people's lives than I had imagined. Though comprehensive national statistics on adoption are virtually nonexistent, we do know that there are six million adopted people in America and that more than 120,000 children are adopted every year. The number of international adoptions in this country has more than doubled since the early 1990s, and 8 percent of all adoptions are interracial.

Today, attitudes about adoption are more open than ever before, particularly among the generation that waited to become parents later in life and who have turned, in record numbers, to adoption as a way of creating a family.

The families that appear in these pages all adopted children younger than six months old. After that period, infants become more attached to their first caregivers, and the separation from them tends to change the nature of their future attachments. Since I wanted to learn how much or little adoption comes into play when all other influences in a family are equal, it was important to have a level playing field—that is, relatively similiar conditions for bonding.

Given issues of privacy, I couldn't represent every aspect of adoption or every adoptive situation. Parents and children experiencing difficulties were uncomfortable speaking publicly for fear of compromising their privacy. But many of the older adoptees I interviewed were quite open about their childhood problems, and whether or not they thought those problems had any connection with being adopted.

Finally, though I interviewed gay and lesbian parents, I did not include their stories, because their children's issues spoke more to their unique family structures than to having been adopted.

To tell the story of the adoptive family, I spoke with parents, children, grown adoptees, and birth mothers in almost every kind of adoptive situation: domestic, foreign, open, semi-open, and closed. I also spoke with families in which there is a mixture of biological and adopted children, which brings still another dynamic to the family.

In open adoptions, which are becoming prevalent today, there is direct contact among birth parents, adoptive parents, and children, either from the beginning or after the adoption. Most adoptions are semi-open, meaning contact between families is made via letters, pictures, gifts, even meetings, all arranged anonymously through an intermediary, such as a lawyer or an agency. Closed adoptions allow for no contact between birth parents and the adoptive family. Most, though not all, international adoptions are closed.

All of these life stories are by turns moving, wonderful, surprising, and always impressive with both individual and universal truths. Nearly every adopted child, young or grown, told me he or she felt "special" because he was adopted. Some children felt the possibility of having been simply rejected by their biological parents, while others understood why their biological parents couldn't raise them. Many parents echoed over and over the words of one mother—"In the end, I think all of us do feel that we got the children meant for us"—though some worried that their children might feel a sense of loss in being adopted.

Grown adoptees described some of the emotional dynamics that occur at different life passages. Many warned that it's not unusual for an adopted adolescent to say, "I don't have to listen to you. You're not my real mother." As devastating as this may sound, each person said he or she had never meant it, but knew it would have the desired effect. These and other observations provided such valuable insights and lessons that I felt tempted to put up a billboard letting all adoptive parents know what might be coming, but not to worry. On that billboard I would also write, "Be honest; your children can handle it."

"I know one thing for sure," said one nine-year-old girl, "your parents are your parents. The people who raise you and take care of you are your parents." In the year and a half I spent meeting and interviewing the people whose stories follow in these pages, I felt fortunate to hear such wisdom and so much good sense about the role adoption plays in a family. My perceptions were widened by seeing the open hearts and minds who created these inspiring and quite regular families, and by the people who grew in understanding because of their particular experience of life. I hope their stories tell you what you need—and long—to know.

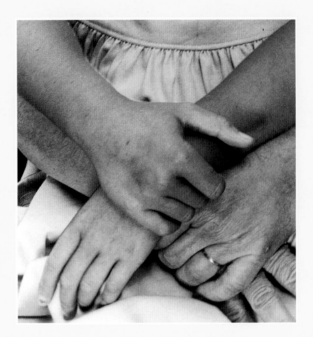

# Mothers
# and
# Fathers

Loving the children they feel were meant for them

# Ileen,
# Mark,
# and
# Alice

Actress Ileen Getz and software designer Mark Grinnell adopted Alice, age eight months, domestically at seven weeks in 1999 in an open adoption. Her birth mother's family is from the Dominican Republic.

## "I don't profess to know how open adoption will work for us; we're a work in progress."

Mark and I were college sweethearts—we met seventeen years ago and were married six years later. I was twenty-six; five months later I was diagnosed with ovarian cancer and had a hysterectomy. Early on Mark thought it would be great to adopt a baby. I had to mourn the loss of our biological child, but at least we were spared the infertility anguish. I think that having absolute knowledge enabled us to deal the hand we were dealt. And now we have Alice.

We tried a private adoption first, but it was a terrible failure; it was actually a scam. Later, we contacted Spence-Chapin. It was terrific to be supported by an agency; they knew all the pitfalls. We put together a book for birth mothers, telling them about ourselves and what we felt we had to offer. The most important thing to us was honesty on both sides. We feared we wouldn't be anyone's first choice; we don't have the white picket fences profile, living in the city and my being an actor. As it turned out, when we asked Alice's birth mother why she chose us, she said it was because we seemed like soul mates. The father of her two-year-old was her soul mate. Alice came about when they took a year apart from each other to decide whether or not to stay together. During that year our birth mom conceived Alice. In the end she got back together with the father of her two-year-old.

I'm glad about the open adoption. I don't profess to know exactly how it will work for us; we're a work in progress. But I'm thrilled I can tell her she comes from a place of strength, and her mom loves her. Mostly, I feel comforted that when she gets older I can tell her, "If you have questions, sweetheart, let's save those for when we see your birth mom." I'm glad her origins won't be a mystery. I don't know whether I'm going to feel wonderful about it the whole time. But we'll take that as it comes.

# Barbara, Steven, Maria, Charlie, and Josephine

In 1994, as a single mother, magazine editor Barbara Jones adopted five-month-old Maria from China. She later married writer Steven Rinehart. In 1999, Maria, age five, became big sister to twins Charlie and Josephine, age six months, biological to their parents.

"When I was single, I thought, 'If there's a living baby who needs a mom, I want to be that mom.' I always saw adoption as a good way to become a parent."

Experiencing birth and being a loving mother bear no relationship to each other. None. My feelings for all my children—my adopted daughter, Maria, and my twins, Charlie and Josephine—have the same amplitude. For a long time, I could not imagine loving any other child the way I loved my first child, Maria, whom I adopted from China. In fact, all during my pregnancy, I had this nagging guilt that I wouldn't love the babies as I loved her. But when my son was born—he was the first one out—he smashed a glass on the other side of which was the way I love Maria. I thought nobody could get there. But he got there. I heard him cry, and I loved him enormously.

I always knew I wanted to be a mother, and when I was single, I thought, "If there's a living baby who needs a mom, I want to be that mom." Adoption was natural to me. Three of my favorite cousins were adopted. I always saw adoption as a good way to become a parent. I didn't have to "come around," as some parents who come to adoption through infertility say they have to do.

The idea of going to China to adopt came upon me after I read an article in *The New York Times* about the baby girls there. I felt a sense of solidarity with them and a kind of sisterhood with their biological mothers. It's ironic: I took umbrage at what was happening—that babies were being separated from their parents because they were girls—but I also felt lucky. I was single, I could support myself, and I had a lot of choices—unlike Maria's birth mother. At the agency through which I adopted Maria, all the adoptive parents had to write a letter to the biological mother. It couldn't actually be sent because there was no way of reaching her. It was simply an excuse to help adoptive parents consider their child's birth parents. I sobbed all the way through writing the letter. I have no desire to erase the reality of this woman. I thought, "I'm getting everything and she's getting nothing, except perhaps the knowledge that she has saved her daughter's life."

Maria was five months old when I first met her, and she was thriving. I felt myself falling for her the moment I held her in my arms. "I'm in love with this child," I thought. Maria has all these qualities that I don't have. She's physically coordinated, and her coloring is just luscious; she's aggressive, and unlike the rest of us, she can talk openly about things that stress her. She was four and a half when the twins were born and she said, "I wish I grew inside you." She just said it. She wouldn't let us skip over her feelings as an adopted rather than a biological child.

I worried when I found out that we were having twins. I worried about Maria growing up in the land of the Caucasian giants. Both my husband and I are tall. Chinese people are not short necessarily, but Maria in fact is not particularly tall. It's ironic because growing up as a tall girl was not always easy for me, and I enjoy the fact that Maria is an average size. I don't necessarily want all my children to have my genetic background. I know too much about those genes.

Because Maria is Chinese, we have a Chinese baby-sitter who is teaching her Mandarin, which I plan to learn as soon as the babies are older. But Maria's relationship to things Chinese is tricky. She resists and rejects it on some level. Since I'm made of eight

different nationalities, like most Americans who've been here for generations, I kind of relish the purity of her Chinese roots. I have to admit that at one time I even felt strongly that she should grow up and marry a Chinese man. But now I laugh at myself. Now I think, "What will be will be what she wants."

Though Maria is beginning to understand some Mandarin, she behaves like many first-generation American kids: She wants to speak only English. I know that her resistance doesn't come solely because she wants to be just like her mom and dad, but because she knows English is the dominant language here. Her Chinese culture class, though, gives her the chance to enjoy speaking Mandarin with her peers. This could all backfire, of course, and she'll be upset with us for making her pay so much attention to her native culture. But if we didn't start helping her to learn about China now, when she reaches the age of eighteen she might turn around and scream at us, "Why didn't you give me Mandarin lessons?" And by then it would be too late.

As adoptive parents, particularly of a racially different child, you have to consider how much attention to draw to the issues of adoption and ethnic differences. It's not only the kids who have trouble with these distinctions, but parents as well. Every year we gather with the eight other families who adopted from China on the same day I did. Some people recoil at calling this day Adoption Day. But for me it's the best day in the world.

It's funny, but at the same time that Maria notices our differences, she also takes it for granted that all kids and families should be just like hers. Last year she attended the Family Center at Bank Street School for Children, a day care center that is diverse in every way. There are kids with a mom and no dad, kids with two moms, biological and adopted kids, kids with every possible skin color. Yet, like all children everywhere, these children have a lot to work out about what makes a family a family. I have reason to believe that some other kids said to Maria, "That's not your mommy, she doesn't look like you." Then again, Maria was taunting a girl who has two mothers, saying, "*I* have a daddy." Traditional ideas of American culture still come in so strong. Perhaps this is a developmental stage. I'm talking about three-year-olds now, trying to figure out what a family is, what the different roles are. And they are being exposed to so many variations nowadays. It's hard for them, but it's great at the same time.

Last year Maria watched some friends at her day care center become older siblings. She said she wanted a bigger family; she wanted a brother and a sister— and a dog. When we told her that I was four months pregnant, she was thrilled. It meant something important to her. It seemed like a tribal thing; she wanted to be part of a bigger tribe. And frankly that's why I wanted to have other children: When I'm a pain in the butt and when I'm gone, she'll have siblings to turn to.

Maria was very jealous when the twins came. We went through a hellish two-week period. She threw tantrums, she cried a lot. She kept telling me to send them away, especially her sister. She wanted the competition gone. She said how much she hated them. She would say

things that were extremely painful to me and for her. She'd say, "I want to look like them, I want to look like you." I would say, "I can understand that, but I love the way you look." It came up over and over again. She was mean, she'd whine. I couldn't bear it. She was enraged. "Why did you have these babies, I didn't want these babies," she'd say. We reminded her that a year before she had said she had wanted a brother, a sister, and a dog. Well, we came up with two out of three.

When she was going through this, I tried to imagine myself what it might feel like to be raised by two Chinese parents who bore two Chinese children. I could see that that might make me feel sad—a broken connection. On the other hand, if they all adored me, that might be cool. I tried to think what it would be like to be the only one who looked the way I looked, and I figured I would probably want what Maria wants, to look the same. The counterbalance, though, is that the twins worship her. She's their big sister. I think she's being seduced by that. It's hard not to feel good when you're their sunshine.

When Maria was three years old, a little boy in her class drowned. That tragedy seemed even more complicated for her than it would have been for a nonadopted kid. She has a keen sense of abandonment and loss. We had to spend a lot of time on it; she kept talking around it. At first she said, "A bad witch is gonna come and take me." She was upset, and it was hard to tell what it was about. Then it became clear that she was upset because she realized that a child could disappear forever. As the year went on, she began to

*"I just know that
if she had grown
inside me, I wouldn't
have had Maria."*

understand that it's extremely unusual for a child to die, but that people *do* die. She said, "One day you're going to die." And I said, "Yeah, but you'll be all grown up. You'll be grown up and maybe you'll have children of your own. And maybe you'll have a husband or someone else in your life." But nothing consoled her. Then one day I said, "Maybe you'll have a brother or a sister," and that consoled her at the time.

We saw that Maria's response to the death of her classmate was an expression of loss for her biological mother. For her there's anger and sadness, and curiosity. Somewhere inside her, Maria seems to know what it's like for a parent and a child to be permanently separated. A child who isn't separated from his or her biological parents doesn't know grief like that. For us that was a terrible sorrow. To love your child more than anything and then to feel that you can't replace something she's lost in her life is very painful. But we are her parents, and I don't think this sadness causes an unbridgeable gap between us. We're very close.

Many infertile women talk about the bond they share with their adopted child because of their mutual sense of loss. Since I didn't come to adoption through infertility, I can't say what that feels like. I did have some miscarriages before the twins, and I had some understanding of that loss, but it's not the same, because I already had Maria. Sometimes I think that coming through the shared sense of loss could be a very good meeting place for a parent and child. When an adopted child comes to her mother and says, "I wish I grew inside of you," the mother may respond, "I wish

you did, too." But I don't. I just know that if she had grown inside me, I wouldn't have had the person who is our Maria, the gorgeous girl with so many wonderful qualities that my genes could never have given her.

My father-in-law died recently. It was sudden and horrible. Someone said that Maria's sadness, or whatever she feels about her separation from her birth parents, is just something about her that's true and sad, just like the death of my husband's father is something about my husband that's true and sad. Loss causes grief, but it's not who you are. It's just one thing in your life.

Most, if not all, of the challenges of being a member of an adoptive family can be dealt with. The real problems come when the whole family is not facing whatever pain comes up. It's not that adoption is not without its challenges. There are bonding issues that come up. But honestly, you don't know what's going to happen with your biological kids, either. Parenthood is always a crapshoot, isn't it? At least when you adopt, you've jumped the hurdles and the unknowns of pregnancy.

We're doing the best we can. We're just parents, and like everybody else we're making mistakes and also doing some things right. The first kid is like the first pancake in some ways. You really don't know what you're doing. It's not like you might not mess up the second pancake, but at least you have a little experience with the batter and the stove temperature. But then again, my twins—my second batch—will never have the undivided attention that Maria received from us, because they are twins and because now we are five.

# Diana, Steve, and Thomas

"Open adoption seemed attractive to us because we felt that it was important for the birth mom to have a sense that the child was okay and for the child to be able to say from the start, 'This is my history.'"

Civil rights lawyer Diana Gilpatrick and government budget analyst Steve Daggett were present in the birthing room in 1996 helping Daria, the birth mother of their adopted son, Thomas, age three, to deliver him (the interview with Daria is on page 123). Theirs is a fully open adoption, with visits from Daria twice yearly and from birth father Damien once a year.

**Diana:** When we first began to explore adoption, we were overwhelmed by all the options. We finally decided to do a private adoption because we wanted to be free of agency constraints. We also wanted to be free to have direct contact with the birth mom and dad. From our own instincts and from everything we'd read, we just knew that it was important for the birth mom to have a sense that the child was okay. We both also felt that it's important for the child to be able to say from the start, "This is my history."

What we originally envisioned was a traditional open adoption where all the parents meet before the birth to discuss and set conditions for how the relationships will work in practice. After the birth, the adoptive parents would send letters and photographs directly to the birth parents twice a year. We would know each other's full names, addresses, and phone numbers, but we wouldn't visit initially—at least not until we had a chance to establish our bond as a family. I feel that if the birth mother is entrusting her child to you, you ought to have enough trust in her to have direct contact with one another.

We're very fortunate in our relationship with Thomas's birth parents, Daria and Damien. I've heard birth parents complain that adoptive parents don't always hold up their end of the bargain and shut the door on them. That's not only painful but disrespectful as well. I understand that some adoptive parents feel threatened by the openness and are afraid of what might happen, that things might change. I guess because we have such a good relationship with our son's birth parents, it's difficult

for me to imagine feeling threatened. But I do recall that early on, when we first saw a film presentation about a very open adoption—the birth and adoptive families were having dinner together all the time—we thought we couldn't do that. We were trying to feel our way through the dark, see what the norms were. Maybe you could call that fear.

I'm a very open person, and Daria is as well. Steve, on the other hand, is more private, as is Damien. For Daria, open adoption was natural. Before Thomas was born, we wrote an agreement together that granted certain rights: visitation rights of birth parents and grandparents, giving gifts, sending photographs. We actually put it all in a letter so that it was enforceable. Our relationship with Daria and Damien evolved to a point of great trust. We really like each other. Almost immediately they became a part of our extended family. With this kind of connection, I can't imagine pulling back and saying we don't want contact.

It is hard to make the leap into open adoption. I think it's the abstractness of it that makes some people nervous. I think all prospective adoptive parents would benefit from going to panel discussions about different kinds of adoption so they could voice their fears to birth mothers directly.

**Steve:** Whatever route you take toward making a family, it's important to be true to your own feelings. One of the issues that always comes up at adoption seminars is interracial adoption. People question whether they can manage the difficulties that racial difference brings to bear. Again, it seems clear to me that you can only do what feels right to you. Going through all these decisions can be an incredible process in which you learn a lot about yourself. You're reacting to something you have no experience with and can't anticipate any outcome from the start. At least Diana and I were on the same page about this. I can't imagine how it would be if we had felt differently.

A lot of people who are adopting go through that infertility trial. We set limits on how far we were going to go early on. We weren't going to do in vitro, and a lot of the treatments short of that were very hard on Diana. It wasn't that difficult for us to give them up. But then we had to live through a painful mourning period. I grieved at saying good-bye to the biological child of my imagination. But the instant we had Thomas, the pain went away. "This is my child," I thought. He's a gorgeous, great kid. He's remarkable. I think whatever kid I had would be remarkable. Thomas just seems more so.

**Diana:** I remember Steve describing the mourning process of giving up the biological child as accepting "the death of the imagined child. You have to put this child to rest, the child who would be the 'perfect replica of us.'" If you haven't gone through this, it's difficult to accept that the child you adopt is as good as the child you might have had biologically. Many of those fears come from feeling that adoption is second best. But you fall in love with your child, no matter where he comes from.

The Christmas when we decided to end our infertility treatments, we sent out a letter to all of our friends and relatives telling them of our search. We explained that we wanted to go the private adoption route, and asked people if they had any leads.

**Steve:** It took about sixteen months. The most frustrating time for me was the many months we had to live through before we got a call. I thought, "When is it going to happen? When?" But we were fortunate in that we belonged to an adoption group and could see it happening for other people. I had a real sense of identification with these friends who adopted, and I felt close to their kids. I still see the children in that group and they're like extended family to us.

Seeing their success made us realize that it could happen. We weren't envious. If it had been another year after they adopted and we still didn't have anything, it would have been different. Every search has its own dynamic.

One of the first calls we received was from the sister of a birth mother. We drove some distance and we planned to meet at a Denny's for breakfast. She never showed up. We felt like, "What are we doing?"

**Diana:** I spent all this time afterward doing a post-mortem, to try to figure out what I might have done wrong. It's hard not to beat yourself up. Now that we're working on adopting our second child, we're learning. We're less likely to beat ourselves up with, "We could have done this. Why didn't we do that?"

Not long after that incident at Denny's, we put together Dear Birth Mom letters with our photos on the back. Our intention was to get this out through as many channels as possible. Since my mother is a Unitarian minister, she goes to many conferences, and she has great ministerial contacts. She went to a conference in Boston and handed our letters out. In a few weeks we got a phone call from a pregnant woman in another congregation. It was Daria. She was the first birth mom we actually met. She was twenty, and Damien, the birth father, was nineteen. We sent our complete Dear Birth Mom package to her, along with a wonderful book on adoption, Lois Melina's *The Open Adoption Experience.* The book was the vehicle that actually helped her get her ideas on the kind of adoption she wanted. Daria started her search with five couples identified through her minister. She got biographical and philosophical information from all of them. She eliminated two who she didn't think would fit in with her needs and desires. She set up interviews with three couples, of which we were one. We met with her and Damien and we really liked them both a lot. We talked for two or three hours. I had this certainty from a dream that her baby was a boy, and she also had a really strong feeling that it was a boy. There was something about that— our being on the same wavelength or something—that brought us together. I just felt it was the right thing. All of our connections evolved. As we got to know each other and as she read through the Melina book, she decided that she wanted an open adoption and a continuing relationship with us.

We decided that Daria would give birth in a birthing center run by nurse midwives. The center was affiliated with a hospital in case of any problems. The delivery happened really fast. I was in the whirlpool tub with Daria helping her, talking to her, telling her to push, massaging different parts of her back that hurt. Then Steve took my place. He was the one who cut the umbilical cord. Right after Daria delivered Thomas, everyone else arrived: Daria's mother and sister, and Damien and his mother. We all left the birthing center two hours after the birth and drove to our house together.

Not everybody could have done this—all of us being

together. It just felt like the right thing to do. We would have felt bad sending them to a hotel. Daria stayed with us for three or four days. She was just such a positive presence. She helped diaper and change Thomas, she held him and tended to him. I breast-fed him by using a supplemental nursing system because I wanted us to have that experience together. Daria said that from the day he was born, she felt Thomas was our child. She really is genuine about that. We're so fortunate.

Daria had read about and wanted to have an entrustment cermony, a public ceremony in which she and Damien would place the baby with us and tell us their wishes for him. We, in turn, would promise them that we would love, cherish, and take care of their baby. We would educate him, nurture him, and do all those things that parents do. We had the ceremony in our church two weeks after Thomas was born.

We're now in the process of trying to adopt a second child. We met one birth mother we really liked, but she wanted a more closed adoption with no exchange of calls and pictures. She wanted to put it behind her— not that you can ever really put it behind you. She also thought that her child would be at a disadvantage if his brother had an open relationship with the birth parents and her child didn't. Birth mothers do think in terms of what is in the best interest of the child. She was right, it would have been hard. The birth parents we're working with now are a much better fit because they want an open relationship.

Thomas's needs are usual for a three-year-old. He loves to see pictures of himself. He loves to hear his life story. He often asks to see his "baby book," which has pictures of me and Steve as babies, our families, our wedding, Thomas being born, and Daria and Damien. When we go look at it together, we tell him who everyone is. It's become a ritual and he can't get enough of it. We tell him that he came out of Daria's tummy. Today, Daria is married to Ted and they have just had a baby, Jacob. Once, when Daria stayed overnight with us during her pregnancy with Jacob, Thomas and I came into her room in the morning and felt the baby kicking in her belly. I said to Thomas, "You were in Daria's tummy, too." Later the next day he said, "I want to go back into Daria's tummy." After that he said, "I have a baby in my tummy!" That's the extent of his three-year-old understanding. Still, having contact with Daria makes it all more concrete for him because he is seeing a tummy that's pregnant, and it's the tummy out of which he came.

We use the word *adoption* very freely with Thomas. He knows he's adopted, but of course he doesn't know what that means.

We have a lot of confidence that he will feel comfortable with it. We have a large circle of friends with adopted children. In his Sunday school, out of a class of ten, three or four kids are adopted. It's going to seem quite normal for him.

**Steve:** I haven't a clue as to how adoption will come into play over time. I haven't even thought very much about it. We have read to Thomas from Jamie Lee

Curtis's book, *Tell Me Again About the Night I Was Born*, and it's a good way to discuss his birth with him. It's really best for him that everyone be very clear.

**Diana:** He's got this beautiful tan skin coloring. He's got Daria's blond hair. He'll probably have different talents than we do. But then I have different talents than my parents, and Steve has different talents than his parents. Thomas's birth father is biracial and his birth mother is white. Thomas doesn't look biracial. We would have been happy no matter how he turned out.

I used to be a die-hard feminist and would never have categorized anyone as having overly gender-based traits. I used to think personality was all nurture. But I've changed my thinking a little. Thomas is only three, and you can already see how he is, a very boyish kid.

**Steve:** I do anticipate that when Thomas is an adolescent, we'll go through some rough passages. All kids go through identity conflicts. They've begun the real process of separating themselves from their parents at that time, and it's hard for them to articulate their true feelings. So he might try to get a rise out of us and say, "You're not my real parents." I know that's very common. I also know that kids don't really mean that. I do think at some point adoption might be an issue for him. But if it weren't adoption at that point, it might be something else. From what I've learned, boys just seem to bury it. I'm hoping our openness will prevent that denial.

# Aubrey, Sonia, and Russell

"The birth father's absence in the adoption scenario creates a sense that fathers matter less. That's why I think it's so very important for the adoptive father to be a really involved parent—to close that gap."

Aubrey Reese, director of children's clinical services of the League Treatment Center, and his wife, Sonia, executive director of Community Impact, adopted Russell, age six, at two months in 1994 in a semi-open adoption. Aubrey is a co-chair of a father's mentoring group at the Spence-Chapin adoption agency.

I have two biological children from an earlier marriage, a son who's fourteen and a daughter who's twelve. Adoption came into my life during my second marriage. I had some reservations about taking that route. I had a lot of fear, anxiety, anger, frustration, and a longing for a biological child with my wife. But there are some ways in which being an African-American family makes it more difficult to talk about the things that come up when we adopt a child from outside of the biological family. In some families there's some question as to whether or not the child will be accepted by the extended family.

Historically, black families frequently have chosen to take care of extended family regardless of their socioeconomic status. We've taken care of the kids who belonged to aunts, uncles, and cousins; another mother or a grandmother who lived down the block would take care of those kids. Explaining adoption outside of the family to someone whose definition of adoption is taking care of their sister's child for a few years is difficult. Often, they can't understand why we would reach out and take care of somebody else's child.

Men, in particular, have a hard time with all of this. Issues of virility, raising "another man's child," and not being a "real father" come up in conversation. I did a lot of soul-searching in those first few months about adopting a child. I had some sleepless nights and some questions in my mind about whether this was the right

thing to do or to spend thousands of dollars to try to have a biological child. As men we're conditioned not to ask for help or support, not to look to other people for comfort when we're in need.

When we were trying to adopt, many of our feelings and experiences were hard to explain to others. It was particularly awkward telling friends we were rejected by one mother for not being Afrocentric enough. When we finally adopted Russell in a semi-open adoption, we were elated.

My wife and I feel strongly that adopted children should be allowed to connect with their birth parents at some point in their lives. It's a difficult process; adoptive parents should talk about it at the beginning, not wait until the child is nine or ten and say, "Oh, my God, we're getting close to the point. What are we going to do?" It's harder for mothers to deal with this, particularly because a mother has this longing to be the "only" mother. I can appreciate that. For fathers, it becomes more of an issue when the kid starts wondering how this baby got here, and that it does take two—when they start thinking about sexuality. We need to get support from other adoptive parents to help each other sort through all those issues before they turn eighteen.

Two weeks ago Russell asked his mom, "Who was I traded for?" like he was a Pokéman card or a baseball player. My wife said, "Traded?" She was ready to give him an explanation when he said, "It's okay, Mom. I just want to go to McDonald's." That says to me that we always have to be prepared for what our kids throw at us. Like my biological children, adopted kids mainly just want to be cared for and loved, and to know that they are home. Adopted children often test the waters to see how far they can push us and still be loved. At puberty, questions of identity can really push children and parents to another level of intimacy or detachment from the adoption issue. Children may feel confused around questions like how much or how little do I want to know about my biological parents? In some way they're looking for closure. Adoptive parents, too, need to sort out their own feelings about being adoptive parents and say, "We've done a good job with our children." Fifteen or twenty years ago, adoptive parents didn't think—let alone speak—about birth parents. I think it's crucial for us to support our children's discovery of their full identity. It's not easy for any of us, but it's right.

The adoption agency at which I run an adoptive father's mentoring group produced a list of children's questions about adoption that came out of an innovative adolescent group. The questions are very revealing about children's fears and concerns. Kids want basic information most of all; they want to know where they came from and under what circumstances they were placed for adoption. Also, their concerns change at different stages of life. It's important for parents to feel secure and understand that these questions don't imply that their children don't feel deeply connected to them, but rather that they're sorting through real life issues. We just have to follow their lead.

It's significant that children generally will search for their biological mothers and not their fathers, at least not initially. The birth father's absence in the adoption process can create a sense that fathers matter less. That's why I think it's so very important for the adoptive father to be a really involved parent—to close that gap. One of the most troubling questions I've asked myself over the last six years is, "Why aren't we talking about Daddy, who—we say, and society says—is an integral part of a child's development?" Traditionally, it's been the mother who has the burden of showing the child how to sort through his or her feelings. It's important to include Dad in the mix. If not, kids, particularly boys, will grow up repeating the same pattern that says, "I have to be concerned only about my wife being a good mother; it's all right if I'm not as emotionally involved on that level." In our mentoring group, we address how crucial the father's role is in a child's development.

A few months ago, Russell shocked everybody while trying to figure out our family's divorce-adoption-two-families situation. He asked his brother and sister, "Okay, you guys have a mommy, and your mommy is *your* mommy. You have a daddy, and your daddy is your daddy and my daddy. And my mommy is not your mommy. But I had another daddy and . . ." He kept on going. We all looked at each other and said, "Okay,

who's going to answer this one?" Part of his support is going to come from his brother and sister. They've been through a divorce; they've got issues to deal with, too. When all is said and done, when you bring your child home, the whole adoption issue becomes secondary. It's just your kid.

"*When all is said and done, when you bring your child home, the whole adoption issue becomes secondary. It's just your kid.*"

# Stephen, Jamie, Sevi, and Madden

"I think all of us do feel that we got the children meant for us. I really believe that along the way we find who we need and who needs us."

Writer Stephen Foreman and actress and children's acting coach Jamie Donnelly are the parents of two children adopted from Colombia: Sevi, age twelve, who was adopted in 1987 at three months, and Madden, age ten, in 1989 at four months. Sevi's interview appears on page 77 and Madden's on page 78.

**Jamie:** More often than not, people who would be happy adopting have enormous resistance at first. When they see families like ours, they often say, "Well that's good for you. . . ." But what they eventually discover by talking to us is that adoption can work for them, too. It isn't like all happy adoptive families didn't have to go through a period of doubt and confusion.

What happens when you decide to adopt is that you move from the uncertainty of "Maybe I'll have a child" to "I'm going to have a child. I'm not sure when, I'm not sure who, but I'll have a child."

People talk about how long it takes to bond with an adopted child. I don't think it's any different than with biological children. There's a lot of free-floating anxiety about adoption. But let's face it, the decision to parent is a big one in itself; there's always the self-questioning. I always knew that I could love an adopted child. I'm afraid of the same things as other parents: What kind of pain will they go through in their lives, and what can I do about that? You worry about the baggage you bring to the relationship. I really don't have strong fears about adoption. Actually, since I was forty when we adopted our first child, Sevi, and Stephen was forty-seven, the only thing I fear as a mother is being an older parent.

**Stephen:** The other day Madden said she felt bad because she was worried that I wouldn't be at her wedding to walk her down the aisle.

**Jamie:** I didn't feel the age issue when I first got my children. But I'm disturbed by the number of people who think it's selfish to raise a child when you're older. It's so ridiculous, but I worry that my children will feel cheated. It certainly gives me more of an incentive to take better care of myself. On the other hand, I think I would have been a terrible parent earlier on. I believe that I'm doing a good job now.

We adopted both of our children from Colombia. When we went to get Sevi, there was a war going on. When we got Madden, I was shaken up by a little boy who was banging on our car window trying to sell us a cigarette. He looked exactly like Sevi. You begin to say to yourself, "Why can't we take care of more of them?"

**Stephen:** Sevi's birth mother came from a very well-to-do Bogotá family. Madden's birth mother, who was of Indian descent, lived in a village in the Andes; she's tall, athletic, red-haired, and beautiful—and she has freckles just like Madden.

I have a fantasy that the errant red hair and freckles can be explained by a Colombian legend that during the Spanish Inquisition, when the Jews were kicked out of Spain, a small group moved down to the jungle and intermarried with the Indians, producing a race of red-haired people.

**Jamie:** Today, Madden is a trendy Los Angeles kid. It's hard to imagine her as the same person who would have lived in the Andes. And though I often imagine my kids chattering to each other in Spanish, neither of them speaks a word of it.

**Stephen:** I don't believe that Madden and Sevi are unduly concerned about their birth parents. And they never talk about their birth fathers. Both have mentioned wanting to go to Colombia, at least once. Finding a birth parent there would be difficult, if not impossible. Attitudes about giving a child up for adoption are very different there than in America. Colombia's is still a Victorian society; birth parents would be less likely to want a child to show up after many years and reveal what happened. There's more shame.

When Sevi was asked to do a report on a foreign country, he chose Colombia, but when Madden was asked to do that same report, she chose Ireland. She's a little more reluctant than Sevi to talk about Colombia. Sevi wants to learn Spanish; Madden hasn't spoken about it yet, though I do think she's proud of the fact that she has some Indian blood. I have heard her talk about it. We don't want to push them toward anything they don't express interest in; we try to take their lead.

*"Let's face it, the decision to parent is a big one in itself; there's always the self-questioning."*

*"When you decide to adopt, you move from the uncertainty of 'Maybe I will have a child' to 'I'm going to have a child.'"*

**Jamie:** Adoption teaches you to notice who your children are, and not to make predictions about them. When you have a biological child, you look at the arch of your child's foot and say, "She'll be a dancer like me." When you do that, you don't always recognize who she is. When Madden was seven months old, she hadn't moved for several months. No moving, no rolling, no nothing. She hung out, all alert and happy, in the Kangerockeroo, taking in everything around her. The doctor said there was nothing medically wrong with her but suggested running tests if she didn't move within two weeks. On the fourteenth day, she rolled. It's as if she was listening and thought, "I'm not taking any tests, I'll roll." Then she didn't roll again, and we decided— with full certainty—that she just wouldn't be a physical person. Madden is now a terrific gymnast!

**Stephen:** Both kids are a lot like each of us in many ways. And, oddly, they both seem to have developed medical problems just like ours. Most adoptive parents are so shocked to see how much like us our kids have become. We are constantly amazed. Both Sevi and Madden are very loving and caring children, and they're completely different from each other. They're proud children, and I want them to continue to feel that way.

**Jamie:** As an adoptive parent surrounded by other adoptive parents, I've noticed one amazing thing: Most of us believe, or have this very strong feeling, that these children were actually meant for us. Whether we decide that we found them or that our children found us, I think all of us do feel that there's a destiny to it.

I've always been aware of the fact that there's the family you're born into and then there's the family you choose. I never felt my children had to be blood-related for them to be mine—it wasn't like it took any adjustment. I really believe that along the way we find who we need and who needs us.

# Brooke, Tony, Josie, and Sophie

"People have this crazy idea that when you adopt, you're just borrowing this child, and he or she won't be connected to you forever. People just don't know that adopted children *do* know who their real parents are."

In 1989, actress Brooke Adams, as a single mother, adopted newborn Josie (who is interviewed on page 73), age ten. She married actor Tony Shalhoub in 1992, when Josie was three years old; he adopted Josie when she was eight. In 1994, they adopted Sophie, age five. Both adoptions are open.

**Brooke:** It may seem funny, but being an adoptive mother, you just know you're totally connected to your child. I don't think I could feel more connected to my daughters if they were my biological children. But for Josie, my oldest daughter, there are always questions, and those questions have changed over time. Josie happens to have a very romantic way of looking at things, and she loves to talk and wonder about life. One day when she was around five she asked me, "What if you hadn't adopted me and you went to my school to pick up your daughter and you saw me and I saw you and we knew that we should be together but we weren't. Wouldn't that be weird?" Amazing question, isn't it?

As a single mother I adopted Josie when she was newborn. The minute she was in my arms, I thought, "She's the light of my life. She's mine." I didn't have a husband then, and though I considered the idea of artificial insemination, when I found out how it's done—that you get a list of donors and their vital statistics: Italian American majoring in math, etcetera, etcetera—I decided I could never have a child that way. You can't find out much more about the donor, and you can never make contact with him. I think it's very important for a child to have the possibility of finding his or her biological parents.

Also, I wasn't so keen on having a biological child. In fact, as a child, I had always hoped I was adopted—though now I see that adopted kids feel they belong

with their parents; they don't see them as "play" parents the ways kids do when they fantasize being adopted. I loved my parents, but they were alcoholics; there was a lot of shame among us because of that. And if alcoholism is genetically based, I certainly didn't want to pass that on to my children.

**Tony:** In 1994, we adopted Sophie. We had tried to conceive, but after a short time when we found it wasn't working, we came to a crossroads. Instead of pursuing fertility drugs or in vitro, we quickly decided to adopt. I didn't feel any need to have a biological child. I'm the second youngest of ten children, I was ten years old when my older siblings began having children. I always felt like I lived in an extended family. Adoption was natural to me since one of my sisters adopted. There was no strangeness about it. Besides, I adored Josie.

**Brooke:** Sophie, who is five, is fantastic, but she definitely has full-blown ideas about things. She's been struggling with the concept of death, for example, since she was two. And she's having some trouble with the fact that she's adopted. Before she even knew what the word meant, whenever we would talk about it, she would cover her ears and say, "No, no." She just didn't want to think about it.

**Tony:** She still doesn't have it clear. When she refers to the birth mother, she calls her "grandmother." Brooke's parents and my parents are not alive, so she's never had grandparents.

**Brooke:** In her imagination, Sophie was with this "grandmother," and spent a lot of time with her, before we came along and stole her away. She has a lot of fantasies about this, some of them very negative toward us. But they come and they go.

**Tony:** She's a real storyteller. Whether you're talking about adoption, sex, or death, she's got a story. In a way, I assume it's her survival mechanism, a way of making sense of life. We slowly try to give her concrete information. We talk to her about when we were in the room where she was born, when we brought her to see her sister, and so on.

**Brooke:** The other day, she said, "Tell me again about the night I was born." I read her Jamie Lee Curtis's book of the same name, and we talked again about the night we took her home. In the beginning, it really bothered me when Josie asked questions about her birth. I remember one really difficult moment when she turned to me and said, "When I was in your tummy . . . "

*"Respecting the truth is the most important gesture*
*you can make for an adopted child."*

*"When you adopt a child, you have to make a leap of faith that everything is going to be okay, not better or worse than if you had a biological child."*

I had to say, "No, you weren't in my tummy." I thought, "Oh, my God, this is going to make her think she shouldn't, or doesn't, love me, or that I didn't do it the right way." Immediately, I told her, "No, you were in somebody else's stomach." Later that day she saw some pregnant woman and said, "When I was in her tummy . . ."

Parents project their worst fears onto their children. But you don't have to; you simply don't have to go to that place where you worry to death about everything. When you adopt a child, you have to make a leap of faith that everything is going to be okay, not better or worse than if you had a biological child. It took me a while to learn this, but after being afraid of Josie's questions, I realized that the most important thing to do is to just answer. You don't have to go into a long embroiled explanation; young kids need simple answers.

I have a powerful belief that it's good when children—any children—face sad thoughts or when they cry about disappointments. Both my daughters are so incredibly emotional. They will get into these crying jags about death. I guess this is the age. When Josie was three she said, "If you die, Mama, I wanna die, too." The other day Sophie started saying the same things—she became totally preoccupied with my dying, her dying, everybody she knew dying, the whole world changing,

and she was just sobbing. Though I can't change this or make it better—it's a fact of life—she got through it. She really enjoyed having a good cry. And she enjoyed being listened to.

**Tony:** Both Josie and Sophie love watching movies about themselves. They can't get enough of it. And I think that's an important thing, particularly for adopted children, because they can see the concreteness of their lives from early on; it grounds them in reality. Also, it's a good thing that they have a lot of friends who were adopted. There are a lot of configurations of family life in Los Angeles, and the kids know it. Difference is acceptable here.

**Brooke:** Still, even with all this openness, other kids will ask if Josie was adopted. My sense of what they're feeling is, "Poor thing." Of course, she doesn't see herself that way at all.

I have friends who aren't as open as I am about adoption. They feel that by not talking about it, they're respecting their children's privacy. I guess I don't see how that works. I see it more as protecting them from the truth. But respecting the truth is the most important gesture you can make for an adopted child. If I started to cover it up, it would seem like a shameful thing to my kids. Of course, there are certain circumstances where it might make sense to keep to yourself. People can be so inappropriate sometimes; they'll just walk up to you and say, "My goodness, your daughter's so blond, where did she get that?" I think it's appropriate to answer—not literally, but in essence—"That's none of your business." That's too intimate a question from a stranger. But I don't think you should say anything or withhold anything that will make your children feel they should keep their adoption a secret.

The whole trick to parenting is the letting go. On every issue, every step of the way, you have to let go of some level of control. You have to learn that things are not necessarily going to work out the way you want them to. It's myself that I have to exercise some control over; I have to let go of my need for my kids to agree or to do most of what I ask of them. When they don't listen, sometimes it takes all my willpower not to want to scream at them.

The thing that drives me crazy about being a parent is this business that "child specialists" insist on—that parents must always be consistent. When you have an absolutely easy kid, you can be consistent. But when you have a difficult child, consistency is out of the question. Some kids are just wild cards, and you have to be flexible with them.

I had an insight one day about why people become so fixated on biological parenting. I was walking with a friend and he was talking about having a baby with his then girlfriend. He said to me, "I have weak knees but my girlfriend doesn't, so I figure our child won't have my weak knees." Thinking this way is not only mistaken, it also may keep biological parents from trying to be the best parents because they think they've already created this perfect being. Then I have friends who say, "No, I don't want to adopt; I want to have my own biological child because I want the child to always love me." They have this crazy idea that when you adopt, you're just borrowing this child and he or she won't be connnected to you forever. They think you'll do all the work and then there'll be no connection. People just don't know that adopted children *do* know who their real parents are. Their real parents are us.

*"After being afraid of Josie's questions,*
*I realized that the most important thing to do is to just answer;*
*young kids need simple answers."*

# Patrice, Allan, Caitlin, and Whit

Film producer Allan and artist Patrice Wachs adopted Caitlin, age nine, at birth in 1989 (her interview is on page 68), and her brother, John Whitman, age six months, at birth in 1999. Both are open adoptions.

"Open adoption has enabled Caitlin to come into her own without these hidden, dark corners in her life."

**Patrice:** There was never just one time that we sat down with Caitlin and told her about her adoption. We talked about it over a period of time, and we continue to talk about it. I once asked her what she thought about her birth mom letting us adopt her. She was so cool. "My birth mother loved me enough to want me to be with people who would love and take care of me," she said. When she was very young, Caitlin had a theory about why she was adopted. Before she was born, she said, she was an angel with one broken wing. I think in her mind that wing represented her foot that was turned in from birth. She said she chose to be born through another woman because I had had so many miscarriages that she knew she couldn't be born through me.

I don't know how that image came to her; we've never had discussions about heaven and hell. But her story is so great because in it *she* made the decision to come to us.

Getting Caitlin was a long, hard journey, but in the end a great one. We'd gone through ten years of infertility treatments. I kept having these spontaneous miscarriages. At that point the idea of adoption scared me terribly. Allan and I couldn't even grasp the concept—that's how far away we were from making that choice.

**Allan:** It was kind of hard to accept that our bodies wouldn't do what we wanted them to do. We tried everything. We started out with a kind of non-Western approach— Chinese herbs, acupuncture. Getting into all the fertility drugs and treatments was counter to all our beliefs. But we did everything—operations, injections, the whole treatment. You never think that you may not be able to have children when you want to.

We're both pretty determined people. Once we set our minds on something, we don't settle for anything less. But not everything in life works out directly. I think people generally get what they want, but not necessarily the way they want it. It took

a long time to get it through my thick head that the end result was what mattered. There was a lot more at stake in raising a child than just biological certainty. Parenting is not simply a product of a blood relationship. In my life I was parented by many people.

In ten years there were a lot of prayers. All I can say is that eventually they were answered. Once we opened ourselves to other possibilities, the child came. But we had to open ourselves up to it. After the child comes, it doesn't matter. It's amazing how all of our preoccupations just washed away.

**Patrice:** One night we went to a meeting for infertile couples. It happened to be a night when everyone brought their children, some of whom were adopted. But the meeting was just too painful for us, and we left. Sometime afterward, without knowing exactly why, we began to look into adoption.

Coincidentally, at around the same time, we heard from a friend who worked in a bookstore in another state. One of her colleagues had a young daughter who was pregnant and thinking about giving her child up for adoption, but she wasn't sure. Allan's response was, "No, no way are we going to get involved with someone who isn't sure." When I called her a month later, she said she had signed up with an adoption agency, and was supposed to decide on which couple she had chosen by the following day. We talked. She liked the idea that we were friends, in some indirect way, of her mother. She felt comfortable with us, that we were similar types of people.

The birth mother has had a difficult life and she needed to heal herself. I think she has. She's married now and is expecting a baby this spring. She feels she's actually broken the cycle in her family of having children young, being confused about life, and raising the child under duress. She's really an amazing girl. She wanted an open adoption, which is what we have. And Caitlin really likes that—the other day when her friends came over and wanted to see pictures of her birth mom so they could see if she looked like her, Caitlin whipped out her scrapbook. It's nice that all of that is available; it's there for her to use as she wishes.

**Allan:** I can see how some people wouldn't want to deal with an open adoption. They'd just want to have their baby and their family and that's that. Not everyone feels comfortable knowing the whole birth family.

We decided to adopt another child because I grew up as an only child and I didn't want Caitlin to be an only child, too. She's a wonderful big sister. One of the things we've always known about her is that she likes to take little children under her wing; she has a lot of compassion.

Caitlin has proven to be a ringing endorsement of the open adoption process. It's enabled her to come into her own without these hidden, dark corners in her life. She doesn't have to wonder about unknowns like "Why didn't they want me? Who are they?" Knowing her birth mother has given her more of a unity of identity. The fact that there's truth in the basic relationships in her life is essential. We all spend our lives trying to answer questions; here's one she won't have to waste her time on. Being open puts the child first, which is kind of a unique point of view as far as history goes, because children have always been getting the short end of things.

I'm not saying that open adoption is right and closed adoption is wrong. It's a question of situation, and also of temperament. I think you have to be careful and very honest with yourself. When you adopt, you relinquish control. The conventional thing about a family is, "No one tells me how to raise my family," but the open relationship changes that a bit; there has to be some acquiescence. But everything has been so positive, we feel this is how it was meant to be.

**Patrice:** Having an open adoption has certainly made Caitlin a more open-minded person. But it doesn't solve every problem. There's still some sensitivity, some avoidance of the issue.

In a lot of ways, Caitlin has had to learn more about life and in a bigger way than most kids who are raised by their biological parents.

As an adoptive parent, you may somehow feel that you're not entirely entitled to your child. This is another reason we support open adoption—to clarify and make concrete the role of the birth mother, and to solidify the permanence of the adoption.

Many grown adopted children are afraid of asking their parents questions about finding their biological mother or father because they don't want to hurt their feelings. They wind up doing things furtively, which I think is painful and difficult for them. They meet their birth parents "undercover" and have secret relationships. I didn't want Caitlin to go through that.

**Caitlin:** I think I know why parents may keep the adoption a secret—they're afraid that when they die their child might think, "Well, I sort of do have another mother . . ." Then that biological mother becomes a substitute for the mother who raised her. But I don't feel like my birth mom is my other mother.

**Patrice:** The possibility of losing your parents is even more threatening in the lives of adopted children. It's remarkable how often this theme comes up in books and movies, particularly in the Disney movies. I guess that it's a metaphor for one of our greatest primitive fears—that we will be abandoned by our parents. After seeing a film with that theme, Caitlin burst into tears, crying, "Am I an *orphan?*" I told her, "No, absolutely not, never." When I told her that there was not one minute that she didn't have parents who were looking out for her, she smiled. Ironically, Caitlin has played the role of an orphan several times. Life is funny, isn't it?

*"Once we opened ourselves to other possibilities, the child came."*

# Barbara, Joel, and Jaime

"When people asked about the differences between my children, I would say, 'We're a family. We're domestic and imported.'"

Adoption lawyers Barbara and Joel Greenberg adopted their son Jaime, age twenty-six, from Colombia in 1973, when he was four days old (his interview appears on page 103). Today, Jaime is a lawyer and a partner in his family's adoption agency. His older brother, Charles, age thirty-two, is owner of a large computer firm. His sister, Kim, age twenty-eight, is a television producer. Both are biological to their parents.

**Barbara:** The search for Jaime started around 1972. At that time we had two biological children. Our daughter was one and our son was six. We actually had a third; we lost him to crib death. We had always thought about adopting. My father, who was a lawyer, had a number of adoption cases in his practice, and I always had a great love and affection for that area of law. I wasn't a lawyer yet, but we were discussing the *Roe* v. *Wade* decision, and my father spoke of how it would impact on his work. Once the abortion bill was passed, there would be fewer children available for adoption. Rather than delay, we looked into adoption immediately. "You already have two children and other people have none," the agencies would say. We went to other people but they wanted a lot of money; the bottom line was dollars, and that seemed unethical to us.

People hadn't started to look abroad at that point, but we thought, "Why not?" Every day I would write five letters to consuls, from Afghanistan to Zaire. The Russians answered, "Come the revolution, we will help you." You never know which door is going to open. We didn't tell our families about what we were doing because we knew we'd be looked upon as maniacs.

When I told Joel that I filed papers in Colombia, he said, "I can't believe you. You don't know anyone who's been there." But we did know this judge who knew that one of the orphanages we were applying to was wonderful. The agencies in Colombia were large charitable institutions that were founded by the crème de la crème of society.

In July 1973, we received letters from two orphanages there. In October, we got a call from one of them—Casa de La Madre—to come down for our baby. I turned to Joel and said, "We have a son." He said, "You're going to believe this?" He was in a panic.

Four days later, we were in Bogotá. Jaime weighed four and a half pounds. His toes looked like little dots. The orphanage brought him out in this gorgeous, lace-covered basinet. He was so cute.

**Joel:** There was another couple from Texas at the orphanage waiting at the same time for the same child, a boy named Santiago. I thought, "What are we doing? Anything can go wrong: We can lose the child; we have no medical insurance." I worried about everything. I got so worked up, I couldn't even figure out how to catch a cab. These other people were totally comfortable, not worried about anything.

**Barbara:** Instead of being presented with Santiago, we were given Jaime. The people at the orphanage assured us that Jaime was more suited to us. But what did that mean? Did they mean our coloring? On what else could they base "suitability"? We didn't care what he looked like. I'm not saying we're great liberals, but we grew up in the Bronx and we were taught not to be racist or prejudiced. Still, this was very new to us. We were urban middle-class Jews, and suddenly we were in this Hispanic culture. But the fact is you really don't know until you're put into that position what will matter to you in the end. Today, at our firm, we get calls from people who want a child that matches, that blends with them. But we never cared.

Once Jaime was home, life was beautiful. We adored our two children, but we wanted a larger family. We wanted some chaos. We learned a lot about ourselves and the outside world when we adopted Jaime. You become a lot more protective of your adopted child. My older son is a computer genius. A teacher of his said, "The world is going to tango, and Charles will do his rumba." He was a challenge to raise. I was not even as protective with my daughter. But both Jaime's adoption and his racial difference made me more aware of his vulnerability. His skin is different from ours. Whenever someone made a remark, as people did many times, I felt an obligation to say, "Oh, yes. This is Jaime, my son. We adopted him from Colombia. Yes, South America." But later, I began to think, "I don't owe anyone any explanations." I realized that people can talk, but what matters is how I handle it. These are my children, and I don't have to identify them. The children would say, "My brother is adopted," and I would correct them and say, "We're a family. We're domestic and imported. His brother and sister came from North Shore Hospital, but he came on the big Avianca airplane." Jaime loved this story.

Joel and I decided to take Jaime to Colombia in 1980, when he was seven years old. Jaime was always very easygoing, but he started to cry. "I'm not going," he said. "Once is enough." He was very angry. We came to understand that he was afraid we were going to leave him there. "We're a family," we told him. "You belong with us and you're not going anyplace."

# Jamie, Christopher, Annie, and Tom

"You never know who your child is going to be regardless of how they come to you."

I know there's no right or wrong way to be a good mother. The essential difficulty, whether you're an adoptive parent or a biological parent, is the self-doubt. I worry that I'm imposing the same preoccupations on Annie and Tom that were imposed on me. I was raised by a task-oriented mother, and I have become a task-oriented adult. "Is this the right thing?" I often hear myself asking. As a mother, ideally I'd like to be enjoying the process and not always looking toward an end result.

My particular brand of self-doubt is more about how to raise my children than about doubting my place as a mother. I've definitely had my vulnerable moments, but I know, regardless of their being adopted, that Annie and Tom are my children—though I'm sure I felt threatened the first time that Annie said she loved her nanny more than me. I probably banged my head against a wall thinking I was a horrible mother. But right now, I think I'm doing pretty well.

I don't believe adoption factors into most of these parenting issues. Quite frankly, I think the lack of a genetic link in an adoptive relationship alters your expectations and allows you to be more open. As an adoptive parent I feel I have more room to give my kids a bit of a break as individuals. I can't project as much of myself onto them. On some level, a biological child struggles more to become an individual. It may be harder to establish his or her own personality independent of whatever traits other family members, even generations back, had in common.

Conversely, if your children are adopted and you don't have a lot of information

about their genetic background, some of their behavior may seem to "come out of the blue." You're dealing a little more on the fly with your adoptive children because you may not know much about their genetic predispositions. There's a tiny bit more of the "Whoa, where did that come from?" with adoption. But *everybody* deals on the fly with their kids. You never know who your children are going to be, regardless of how they came to you.

There is one issue, however, about adoption that makes me very sad. And I'm reluctant to even articulate it because I feel as though I'd be predetermining my children's fates, and it may just be my own fear, my own projection. But I worry that adopted children might be more lonely. I think the fundamental abandonment perhaps creates a loneliness, a feeling of disconnectedness from the world or like there's a big missing piece. I don't even know if it will be true for Annie or Tom. And I know that children can feel this way even when they are raised in their biological families. But I understand loneliness, and it concerns me.

My new book contains two songs written by one of our dearest friends, David Nichtern, that speak so

movingly about what it means for parents to take a child into their lives. One of them, *The Wind Brought You to Me*, is kind of an anthem.

When I read the lines to this song, I felt a lightning bolt go right through me to my core. It's an amazing gift that this man gave to us—as simple and right as I've ever heard anyone explain what it means for me and my husband to have Annie and Tom in our lives, and what it is for any parent to bring a child into their lives.

Tiny victories and tremendous losses—that's what family means to me. All the good stuff comes from those victories; they're small epiphanies where you learn something new and important by going through something difficult. Recognizing those moments is what makes you feel vital and successful as a parent.

Unfortunately, where I want to be as a mother and where I am at certain times often seem to be diametrically opposed. I know in my heart it's an ongoing process, that you don't just arrive fully formed as a good mother. What we're talking about are the universal struggles of being a parent. You learn to be one.

*"On some level, a biological child struggles more to become an individual."*

*To keep you safe and warm*
*the wind brought you to me.*
*To shield you from all harm*
*The wind brought you to me.*

*On and on*
*In a circle yet unbroken,*
*to carry on like a dandelion*
*the wind brought you to me.*

*To kiss and hug you tight*
*the wind brought you to me.*
*To keep me up all night*
*the wind brought you to me.*

*On and on*
*Cause the story's still not finished.*
*So carry on like a sailing ship.*
*The wind brought you to me.*

*And when you are full grown*
*the wind will speak to me.*
*And tell me how you are*
*even far across the sea.*

*On and on*
*In a circle still unbroken,*
*you'll carry on*
*When you are full grown*
*the wind will speak to me.*

# Myra and Anna

"I hope when Anna gets to high school and people choose up sides by ethnicity, she'll know in her bones that everyone within these groups is only an individual in an ethnic outfit."

Writer and professor Myra Goldberg and physicist and environmentalist Marvin Resnikoff adopted tap dancer and soccer player Anna, age ten, domestically at birth in 1989 in an open adoption. Anna is biracial. Her parents are now divorced.

In making a decision like adoption, it's important to know what you can and can't do. By the time I went through a series of decisions—about finding a man to have a family with, about various fertility procedures and how far I would go toward getting pregnant—adoption seemed like more of a possibility. I had gone quite far toward conceiving, including getting up early in the morning to travel some distance for some famous doctor's treatment. But adoption has fairly quickly come to mean having a real baby instead of hormones that might or might not have produced a child. Still, had I not gone down that road, even partway, I might not have come to adoption. On this path I met Marvin, who became my husband, and he was open to everything, which I am still grateful for.

It was comparatively easy to decide that we would adopt here in the United States instead of internationally, because even poor people here probably have better medical care than in many areas abroad, and because immigration bureaucracies and even more forms seemed daunting. More important, I had some feeling about offering a home to someone from *this* country. I didn't care about the race of my child, but since we became an interracial family, my place in society has changed, and so has my consciousness.

Before doing this interview, I asked Anna if it was okay with her. "Well," she said, "as long as I know the writer and I get to see the book." I thought those were reasonable criteria for trust. In a sense, they mirror what I felt about her birth mother: "I like this woman," I thought, when I spoke to her on the phone, and that seemed like a basis for making this decision. Kathleen sounded like a person I could connect with and tell my daughter about with respect and pride.

Obviously she had to trust me in far more important ways than I had to trust her. Some years after Anna was born, Kathleen called me at work. We had spoken occasionally before, but this time it was less formal, more intimate. She was eaten up, she said, because she thought Anna might think badly of her, might think she'd made the decision to put her up for adoption carelessly. At first I was uncomfortable: "Why is she telling me this? Can't she talk about her anguish to someone else?" Then I realized that in this situation, I was the person most connected to her and, in a certain sense, most sympathetic. Now she wanted me to tell Anna that she had made this decision with great pain and that she did it in order for Anna to have a better life than she could offer.

Sometime later, Kathleen sent Anna a Barbie doll and a whole collection of family pictures. On the back of the pictures of cousins and aunts and even a missing grandfather were notes that said things like "Love from your cousin John." I said to Anna, "It must be nice to know that all these people care for you." "Oh," said Anna, who is a realist, "they probably wrote those cards because Kathleen asked them to." Cold eye, warm heart, someone once said about the writer Chekhov. Anna is a lot like that.

I think adoption is a puzzle for Anna and will have different meanings over the course of her life. She thinks a lot about babies, what age you should be when you have them, and whether she will adopt or not. Recently, an ad came on the radio about how many teenagers get AIDS every day. I must have looked upset, because she said, "Mom, you don't have to worry. I'm going to adopt."

In some ways adoption is a minor character in Anna's and my life story. Most of the time it feels as if we are struggling with what everybody in families struggles with—how to feel cozy and give each other some room, how to enjoy each other, how to function as a team, how to say what "enough" is.

If there's one thing Anna has to grapple with, it's our divorce, which is not about adoption but about her daily life. She sees her father every day because he picks her up and they go to school together. On Friday nights she stays at his house, and on Saturday they go to soccer. They have a lively, independent relationship. She knows she has his love. But she basically lives with me, and that's quite different from living in a family with two parents. One of the less obvious changes is that we are roommates and friends as well as parent and child. There is a playmate side to our relationship, and we have to do a lot of negotiating about whose music to listen to and who picks up the towels from the floor. It's harder to come on as an adult if you have just been playing tag. But, in many ways Anna is quite grown-up. She has watched me cope with things one-on-one. She can still pull her kid things, but often she has a pretty insightful explanation for why she does what she does.

I had thought that by adopting a child, I would avoid that classic parental mistake that your child is like you, or worse still, *is* you, and needs what you need, or needs what you didn't have. Actually, I have gone through all the same stages as every other parent—overidentifying with her, wanting her to be good at things I'm bad at, wanting her to be good at things I'm good at, worrying about her making her way through the world before she's out of elementary school. These family issues—sameness and difference—are available to everyone in every kind of family.

I think the sense of contingency—that it could have happened differently—is in the background of any adoptee's life. One of Anna's favorite questions has always been, "If you adopted someone else, would you love her as much as me?" Sometimes this imaginary competitor is a little blond girl. "No," I say, "because I would always know that you were somewhere in the world and that you were the one for me." Then she laughs and laughs. "Mama, that's stupid. You wouldn't know about me. Of course, you would love this other girl." But I insist. I think I'm right to insist that this bond is more than chance. Or that the love in it makes the chance less important. Also, I hear this question as something from a fairy tale, as a test.

It's not only adoptees who question the solidity of their relationship to their parents. We've all had "maybe I don't belong with these parents" fantasies. I remember my mother telling me that she decided as a child that she'd been left on the doorstep by gypsies, that she had another real family somewhere. Anna

has several candidates for her fantasy "family." In the rock-bottom sense, the people who put you to bed and get you up in the morning and show you the part of the world they know are your family. They are the people who yell at you and the people who love you.

People ask about being an interracial family. Or they don't ask. Part of what has happened in opening up my family this way is that my loyalties, my sense of who I feel connected with, has changed. I feel much more connected to African-American and Hispanic people than before, much more aware of how pervasive racism is. It's my kid, after all, who is going out into a world in which people like her will not be seen

for who they are. I have become compulsive about telling her teachers how smart she is, what excellent writing she has done, and putting her failings in the context of her gifts. Every parent needs to do that, but more so for me.

Before I put her in private school, I could see that she was being overlooked. The private school she goes to was founded during the civil rights movement as a serious commitment to racial tolerance, so she is growing up with seventeen kids who are black, white, Hispanic, mixed, adopted, whatever. And that makes it harder for ethnic generalizations to exist. There aren't enough white kids to say, "White kids act like this." Instead you say, "Jeff is a baby." Or "Susie always wants what I have for lunch." I hope when Anna gets to high school and people choose up sides by ethnicity, she'll know in her bones that everyone within these groups is only an individual in an ethnic outfit.

That doesn't mean these ethnic outfits don't serve some purpose. Anna sees herself as African American rather than as biracial. She loves clothes, complex hairdos, and shoes. Once she said to me, "White people don't care what they look like." I could see how, given my bohemianism and that of my white women friends, she could say that. We don't "dress." Once she called me "white girl." I had one of those moments when I thought, "I could laugh at this or I could take this seriously." I said, "We never tease people about things they can't do anything about." I probably should have gone for the laugh. What's moving to me and important is that Anna has an expansive sense of what her identity is. More than anything, I credit her baby-sitter, Madalyn, for this. Madalyn is Dominican and looks a lot like Anna. She takes Anna to her family, who are black and white and biological and adopted and fostered. Madalyn wears tight jeans and hoop earrings and platform shoes and looks fabulous and sexy and wants to get a Ph.D. in neurophysiology—and she will. She has such a complex identity herself and such broad social boundaries that she says implicitly to Anna, "You can be who you are and wear what you want, and be street smart, and be a scientist." Whereas in my generation, I didn't know you could wear high heels and be a scientist.

Anna is making herself up. That's what all kids have to do, even if their families look ordinary. And it's very touching to see how kids become themselves in the world. The culture you hand them doesn't work without all kinds of modifications for the next go-round. Anna is a rich, idiosyncratic person, not predictable in any sense. It will be her job to teach people how to see her. It's a huge thing, to have to face people who assume they know who you are, in the most shallow sense, and to be able to say, "No, I am this and this and this," and not allow yourself to get smaller to suit their uninformed ideas. I'm not a black mother and I haven't experienced what Anna's going to experience, so I can't share that with her. I've never felt overt racism.

When Anna was a baby, we were always asked questions about our relationship to each other. No more, for some reason. I'd like to think that's because it has become, by the gestures and chatter and laughter and irritability between us, totally obvious.

# Mark, Hannah, and Sarah

"Life is a gamble—having a child is a gamble—and you have to take a chance. But sometimes you just know things are going to work out."

**Mark:** Getting Sarah was truly a miracle. At first, we tried putting ads to birth mothers in different newspapers, but only a few people responded. Then, out of the blue, someone we had been in touch with called and told us our baby had been born.

It still seems like a miracle because Hannah had to do so much, so quickly, to make certain that we got Sarah. We had to get everything together in two days! We weren't sure that we would get all the papers in time, but Hannah turned on a dime. She was so assertive and so determined; it was amazing. She went to family court to get all the papers. She pulled every string and did everything possible—and impossible—to get what was needed.

**Hannah:** We had to fly and then drive for two hours to get to the hospital where Sarah was born. We brought along a car seat, a blanket, and some clothes; that's all we had time to gather. There was this absolutely miserable snowstorm; trucks were jackknifed all along the highway. We had to meet the lawyer who was to turn Sarah over to us after we met with her birth mother. You can imagine how terrified we were of being late. Life is a gamble—having a child is a gamble—and you have to take a chance. But sometimes you just know things are going to work out.

Sarah's birth mother was a bright, beautiful woman who cared deeply about this baby. She even insisted on having legal papers that would indicate who would be Sarah's guardian if something happened to us. She didn't want to be there when Sarah was given to us because she was concerned about becoming too attached to her. So Sarah was looked after for several hours by all the nurses in the maternity ward.

Mark Kinn, a physician, and his wife, Hannah, executive director of the League Treatment Center, adopted Sarah, age ten, at birth in 1989 in a semi-open adoption. Sarah's interview appears on page 84.

Mark: During that time, we waited for Sarah in a parked car in this Stop & Shop across from the hospital. The lawyer's wife handed us this bundle, which we unwrapped like the petals of a flower. When I saw Sarah's face, I just fell in love with her. She was sleeping. We couldn't believe we finally had her.

There was klezmer music playing on the radio in the hotel where we spent our first night with our new daughter. When we came home with Sarah, we turned on the same music and danced around the living room with her in our arms. We were enraptured. Klezmer has become our theme music for her, and we play it on every special occasion.

Hannah: We told Sarah her birth and adoption story when she was around three years old. We described how we went through the snow, and all about the policeman named Butch who helped us. She loves the story. I was always waiting for her to ask questions about her adoption, and when she finally did, at the age of four, she asked, "What kind of car did you rent?" Later, she asked us about her birth mother: "Was she very young?" and "Why did she give me up?" We told her that she was around nineteen and without a husband. She wanted the best for Sarah: to have a family who could give her all the opportunities for a good life that

she couldn't. We explained that she had thought very carefully about who would raise her, and had arranged, a long time before she was due to give birth, for her baby to be adopted. Sarah wanted to know if the birth mother was there when she was given to us and who took care of her before that happened. We told her the nurses were with her because her birth mother didn't want to get too attached to her. She felt this would be the best way for her to give Sarah to us.

Sarah has asked, "Who do I look like?" and I've said, "You look like your aunt Linda, who also has blond hair and blue eyes."

Mark: I've also told her she looks like her birth mother. In the beginning, when we first explained everything in a way she could understand at such a young age, Sarah always loved this *Sesame Street* book about adoption. It spoke of how adoption was just another way to make a family. And she accepts that. I've told her different things about her roots at different times. One time, when the Yankees were playing at a stadium on the shores of one of the Great Lakes, I told her, "That's where you were born, on the shores of a Great Lake."

Hannah has written to her biological mother, so we do have a connection to her. Sarah has expressed an

*"Sarah is the greatest manifestation that we are lucky people."*

*"We're a family. I'm the only person she'll ever call Daddy,*
*and Hannah's the only person she'll ever call Mommy."*

interest in knowing about her, and in meeting her. We've told her that we'll arrange for them to meet when she's eighteen.

**Hannah:** Whenever I feel bleak about something, I know I can't feel sorry for myself because we have Sarah, and I feel so blessed. I'll never forget that Sarah's first word was *light,* because she is the light in our lives.

**Mark:** Sarah is the greatest manifestation that we are lucky people. We were reluctant to adopt another child for fear that the odds of having a child who is as warm, smart, and beautiful would be so small that we couldn't imagine it. We raised the question with her about a brother or sister, and she said, "Yeah, it would be good to have a sister, but then you'd have to share your toys with her." And she was concerned that a sibling would take our attention away from her, which is a natural fear.

**Hannah:** I almost feel we can be more boastful about Sarah because, when we do, we're admiring her for herself, not as an extension of ourselves. She is this wise person who we've watched unfold. She has filled our lives so much that I say to Mark, "What did we talk about before we had her?"

I do feel that in being a family, we've become like each other. Among other things, Sarah's developed Mark's exquisite sensitivity to smell, and they both love sports. I paint and Sarah paints. She touched me one day when she said, "Mommy, when I grow up, I want dark curly hair like yours." And I said, "Sarah, all my life I wanted straight blond hair like yours."

**Mark:** We don't necessarily take credit for her great gifts, so we can more easily nurture and appreciate her as an individual. Yet on the other hand, if she does negative things that remind us of ourselves, we feel guilty. We think, "Uh-oh, she learned that from us." Obviously, both her gifts and her problems grow from our lives together.

**Hannah:** One of the great things about living where we do is that there are so many adopted children. Sarah went to a preschool that was run by a woman with two adopted children of her own. Adoption is very common, very familiar in our community. I was walking home from preschool one day with three little girls, all of whom happened to have been adopted. They were chattering away, and one girl said, "We're all adopted." And another girl said, "Yeah, and we're all allergic to the cold."

*"I almost feel we can be more boastful about Sarah because we're admiring her for herself, not as an extension of ourselves."*

**Mark:** Sarah knows about her background—her part Native-American heritage, among other things. She also knows that she was converted to Judaism as an infant. She loves her Hebrew name. She once said, "Well, I'm not completely Jewish, and I want to have a Christmas tree," so we compromised and put up Hanukkah lights. We've always told her, "If you want to choose not to be Jewish when you grow up, that's up to you, but I think you'll be Jewish because we're a Jewish family. This is how our family was made." She hasn't referred to her adoption very often, but she has said, "Because I'm adopted, I feel a little different." She asked us if we were adopted, too. I said, "No, I wasn't adopted, and the truth is I can't understand exactly what it's like for you. It's your special thing." But in some ways, because my own background was so radically different from my parents', who were Holocaust survivors, I feel I can identify with her experience: that we have differences but that's all right because we have similarities, too. We're a family. I'm the only person she'll ever call Daddy, and Hannah's the only person she'll ever call Mommy.

# Mitchell, Joann, Jared, Kayla, and Whitney

## "A family is a family. It doesn't matter how it comes to us."

Stockbroker Mitchell and teacher Joann Goldman adopted newborn Jared, age fourteen, in 1985 in a closed adoption. They gave birth to Jared's younger sisters, Whitney, age ten and a half, in 1987 and Kayla, age eight and a half, in 1990. Jared's interview appears on page 81.

**Joann:** It's very interesting to talk to other people about adoption because when we decided to adopt, I could not conceive of having any problems with it. A family is a family. It doesn't matter how it comes to us. On the other hand, Mitch was apprehensive. I recall him asking, "Will I be able to love this child?" and I said without a doubt, "Sure. Yes, you can."

**Mitch:** I did have some problems with it. I think generally men have more of a problem with adoption than women. One of the fears—and I'm not saying it's rational—is that you'll be perceived as less of a man—a potency problem. "What's the matter, shooting blanks?" You think that's what people are thinking. Then blame can come up as an issue in a couple. Whose fault is this? But it was never an issue with us. You just say it wasn't meant to be.

I also had some problems about adoption from a moral standpoint. It seemed unethical that I should be able to have a child because I had the money. I was also concerned that there was this gray market in children. But I overcame that.

**Joann:** Mitch was also afraid that he would fall in love with the child and that the birth mother might change her mind. We hired a private adoption attorney. She was very progressive and strongly conveyed that this would be done in a totally ethical, legitimate way. We went through the various interviews, examinations, and paperwork. I remember our attorney saying, "Don't ask me for a blond-haired, blue-eyed child because people do ask and I can't deliver this like a takeout order."

Not too long after, our lawyer called us for a meeting. First she asked, "Would you like a son?" And I had to laugh. "Has he got two eyes, a head, and a full set of toes?" "Yes," she said. "Okay, I'll take him." Jared was two days old when we adopted him. Once they put him in my arms, there was not a doubt in my mind that he was mine.

**Mitch:** I lost it when the attorney came out carrying the baby and handed him to Joann. I just started crying. It absolutely cleared up the love issue. I fell for him immediately.

The support that you get from your family is really, really important. I had a friend who didn't get any and it was painful. Her parents always said to her, "The child will never feel like yours." This couple went through torture. It's heartbreaking. But you know, most likely if they had adopted, her parents would have overcome their prejudices once they saw the child, just as I did.

**Joann:** We were so lucky that we never heard anything like that. "Go and get a child," my parents told us. "Why are you breaking your hearts?" Stay away from close-minded, negative people who will turn you away from adoption.

**Mitch:** Joann's grandmother had a problem with Jared. She'd refer to him in the third person. So we avoided her. I used to say, "You have lost out on a wonderful experience."

**Joann:** To tell you the truth, most of the time I forget that I didn't give birth to Jared. People sometimes ask me about his birth and I say, "Oh, yes, I carried him—I carried him in my heart." It's odd, but in some ways I felt more strongly about him at the beginning. I love my girls to death, and we all know that. But it was such a struggle to get Jared, I had such a sense of the miraculous when we got him.

**Mitch:** When Joann later became pregnant, I didn't want to know the gender beforehand. I thought, "I have a son and I love my son. I want to have a girl." Partly I was afraid of having another son because I thought that it would cause some competition or conflict. I didn't want to feel, "Now I have a 'real son.'" Do I believe this? No. And I can't believe that I was ever worried about it. But you go through these things. You have natural doubts.

**Joann:** We never made adoption an issue. I can't say I haven't worried about what adoption was going to mean to Jared down the road. What will he want to know about his biological mother? I always wanted him to know everything about himself. I didn't want him finding things out from other people. I have told Jared the story of his birth as I have told my other children.

I chose not tell anyone that Jared was adopted during the first few years of school because I didn't know what kind of student he was going to be and I didn't want the teachers to start out with any preconceptions about him. But I told Jared, "If you want to tell others that you were adopted, fine, that's your choice. If you don't want to tell, that's fine, too." I wanted Jared to be Jared. I didn't want anyone to feel sorry for him. If he was going to be mischievous, it's because that's who he is. If he was going to be creative and wonderful, that's because of him and not because of his background. He has to be responsible and take the consequences.

**Mitch:** When you adopt a child, you end up talking a lot about heredity versus environment. Nature versus nurture. Though I'm a big believer in environmental influence, I know that certain traits are going to be there from the start.

**Joann:** If you take care of them well, most children will turn out okay. It's dangerous for parents to worry themselves to death about who their children will be and who they take after. As an adoptive parent, you have to be careful not to project your insecurity and fear of what might separate you from your adopted child. You can't worry that he does that and we don't. When he was born and I could see that Jared had his own personality and some of those traits weren't ours, I understood that he has his own genetic material. Jared is definitely his own person. In fact, he's very gifted.

There are things that my biological girls do that we don't do and I don't think, "Where did they get that?" They do that because they do that. Same with Jared. I don't wonder about that.

Since Jared was our first child, and an adopted child, we tended to bend over backward for him. I thought, "I better do a good job." At first I tried to save him from having any problems, but then I understood that he needed to learn by making his own mistakes. It's interesting to think that we might have been different as parents if we'd had biological children first. Raising an adopted child teaches you a lot about letting kids be who they are.

A lot of adopted children wait until their parents have passed on to find their birth parents because they don't want to hurt their parents. And I can't say that it wouldn't hurt in some way because I'd wonder what I did wrong. Adoptive parents have fears, all kinds of fears, including their own self-doubt as to whether or not they deserve to be the true parents of this child. You're harder on yourself. Still, I always say, "What makes a mother a mother isn't that she's the one who carried you in her stomach. Anybody can have a child, but not everyone can be a mother." And I firmly believe that. I'm the one who cared for him, cried with him, and laughed with him. My love for him is so strong, I

*"Anybody can have a child, but not everyone can be a parent."*

think it would disturb me to find his birth mother. I wouldn't want to share him. But I have to say that as I mature and become more secure, I feel more open to it.

When I was younger, the idea of the birth parent really frightened me. I didn't want someone knocking at my door after eight or ten years and saying to Jared, "Hi, I'm your mother." "Excuse me," I'd think, "no you're not. I'm the person who has earned the name mother." The media stories don't help; you don't read about all the good, successful adoptions. Fortunately, as the kids get older and more secure, I have become more secure in our relationship, and I don't fear the birth parent as much.

**Mitch:** At times we do actually worry that Jared doesn't talk about adoption enough, that he doesn't ask more questions.

**Joann:** I once asked him, "Why don't you ever ask me about your adoption?" He said because he never thinks about it. It bothered me somehow that he doesn't. I thought at the very least he might wonder who he looks like. But he said he didn't.

During his bar mitzvah speech he said something about being adopted. I was so proud and glad for him that he felt comfortable enough to speak so publicly about being adopted.

**Mitch:** There are two ways to look at everything: half full or half empty. There are adopted people who feel inadequate because they believe they were given up for

lack of love. Maybe their parents put it to them that way, as a negative. We explained to Jared that we were all given this gift, this special person, and that his birth parents cared about him, too. We can only presume that it all worked out the way it did in order to give him and us this good life together.

**Joann:** We didn't want to raise an only child, so we wanted to adopt a second child. Then when I became pregnant, I told Jared, it was meant to be that he was my oldest and my first. He was really comfortable with that idea. I thought again about the insecurities that could come out. How would an adopted child and a biological child accept each other? But it never became an issue between them. I can't stress enough how important it is to tell children their birth story and to tell them the truth.

**Whitney:** I once made fun of Jared for being adopted. And after that I felt pretty bad. I was angry at him. What do you say to your brother when you're angry at him? You just say mean things. I think he felt very bad. I don't really treat him different now. We're really equals. My friends know that Jared is adopted. I think it's cool.

Sometimes I think about it. I don't have any friends in school who are adopted.

**Joann:** I was very careful when I was pregnant with my daughters. I ate well, I carried well, and did all that I had to do. I had amnio and everything. We had all the guarantees in the world. And—boom—we had a genetic issue: hearing impairment. I do think that having gone through the trials of adoption, and all the questions it brings, made it easier for us to accept this challenge for our girls. It could have been worse, much worse. This is nothing. Dealing with life when it is not simple makes you stronger. My daughters have dealt with their problems admirably, and I'm so proud to be their mother. They're very special people.

**Mitch:** If I had had a biological child first, I don't know if I would have said, "Let's adopt if we can't have another child." I can tell you honestly that I would have thought, "It's not meant to be. God gave me this one child." I don't know if we would have made that leap. I don't know if it would have been enough to overcome my doubts. Now, knowing how wonderful it is, I wouldn't hesitate.

*"Raising an adopted child teaches you a lot about letting kids be who they are."*

# Esther, Peter, and Noah

## "We're very aware that no matter what circumstances result in your becoming a family, if it works out, it's kind of a miracle. Who knows why?"

**Esther:** In some ways we feel freer as adoptive parents and think Noah is freer, too. He doesn't have to be a chip off the old block. Adoption is less laden, at least for us, with all those expectations that your child reflects who you are.

**Peter:** Every child is entitled to his own self, but in adoption it's more concrete. Then, over the years, when we got close and really became a family, we began to take on some of each other's habits. We have definitely merged more, which changed my perception of his independence. It's ironic that now that he's going into adolescence and becoming more of a separate person, now that he's become such an essential part of my life, of my being, I've actually lost sight of his separateness—just when he needs me to accept it.

**Esther:** Raising a child, the decisions you make, the way you feel about how you're doing, are all based on your projections onto your child of how you feel and what you want, instead of what he feels and what he wants. Whether children are biologically yours or adopted, you project on to them everything you think, and know, and fear. We did that when Noah was little. If Peter was cold, therefore Noah was cold. If I was hot, Noah was hot. Then the debate became, "Is he cold or is he hot? Does he feel what you feel or what I feel?" By being so close to you, he becomes like you. Then you may start projecting more intensely. It's so clear what Noah's picked up from us.

Writer and labor union cultural director Esther Cohen and documentary editor Peter Odabashian adopted avid skateboarder and artist Noah, age thirteen, from Chile in 1986, when he was six months old.

If you ask him a question and he stares at you blankly, that's me. It drives Esther crazy in me, and now it drives her crazy in Noah. And now, for the first time, I can see it in myself, and it drives me crazy, too!

**Peter:** Adoption does come into play in subtle ways. For one, you don't have the same expectations at the beginning that you do with a biological baby, which is "Aah, Bess looks just like Grandma Rose." When they're biological, you see yourself in them right from the beginning. With an adopted kid, you only start doing that when they're older. You see that he has learned the traits of your grandmother through you.

**Esther:** I was raised with my biological parents, and we had little in common. My interests were and are completely different. My mother and I, who grew up looking at all the same things from the age of zero, saw every single thing completely differently. Our attitudes, our response to things had very little to do with some blood connection. I knew that as a kid.

I don't think either of us had any expectations from the beginning that Noah was going to be like us or not like us, or anything in particular. We only knew he was going to be a person who we were lucky enough to live with. We were committed to taking care of him in the best way we could given the fact that we were parents who had parents who were problematic because they were our parents. The adopted aspect of our raising him doesn't play a big role.

**Peter:** I grew up as the "other," for very different reasons than an adopted child. I was from an immigrant family that was relatively less educated and less wealthy than everyone else in town. My parents were Armenian and I was first-generation American. We were isolated by religion, culture, and money. Part of the reason I was attracted to and married Esther was because she was clearly never going to let me live my life in isolation the way I was raised to live.

**Esther:** I grew up in quite a tribal situation, too. We were Jews in a town that wasn't Jewish. Peter and I decided very early on in our relationship that we wanted to live in a very open, universal way where there was no idea of an "other," someone who was different, outside of our culture.

**Peter:** Ironically, Noah has embraced this idea of the "other." His idea about how he is different is not so much about being an adopted kid as it is about being an immigrant, which he's very proud of. Perhaps he feels that affinity with me and my immigrant status. But I think he also identifies with the other kids in school from immigrant backgrounds. Maybe as much as half of his class are immigrants' kids.

**Esther:** His first friend at school was a Japanese boy who couldn't speak English. Now he has a Brazilian friend who can't speak English. He'll always be friends with kids who can't speak English. Noah wrote a piece about his notion of tolerance and what intolerance can lead to. He said that his idea of life is to be open to the differences in others. It made me really happy. This is a recurrent theme in Noah's life; the theme of his school is tolerance.

**Peter:** I grew up feeling bad that I was the "other." I didn't know you could flaunt your differences. I think Noah likes that. He likes being the rebel, being different. It's not artificial. It's natural to him. I tried to conform when I was a child, but it didn't work. I never worry about Noah's unhappiness about being different.

**Esther:** I think because of my sensitivity and Peter's to this notion of being ghettoized, we've tried to live with a more fluid, open idea of family. And that's where Bruce and Cliff come in. For us, friends became family. We couldn't speak of our lives as a family without talking about Bruce and Cliff [pictured to Esther's right on page 61]. The year before Noah was born, Peter and I, Bruce, and Cliff all bought an old house in a small town in upstate New York. Since the day we brought Noah home, Bruce and Cliff have been essential people—no less than family—to him. They were the ones who met us at the aiport when we arrived from Chile with Noah in our arms. Noah would tell you they were his premier baby-sitters. We travel together, eat together, spend holidays together. We know the friends and women who have moved in and out of their lives. We've all been inseparable since college—I went to school with Bruce, and Peter with Cliff and I can't think of Noah's childhood and life without seeing them there, always.

Much is made of the birth mother relationship, and I think it's important, but also sometimes exaggerated for reasons other than the inherent blood connection. I think the reunion with a birth mother is so intense, so powerful because of the romance of loss, not necessarily because there would have been a great relationship. You long for what you don't have, and many of us feel that way at times. It's so complicated.

There's definitely a karma aspect to adoption, and it probably runs both ways. As an adoptive parent I do feel that things have worked out the way they should. In Yiddish we say, "It's *bashert*"—it's "meant to be."

**Peter:** As far as the birth parents are concerned, I have to ask: Does the history of that body out of which the child was born have as much to do with that child as the child's own social history? I don't think there's any way you could say. I think it borders on racism to think that biology is destiny.

Noah will never be able to answer the "what if" aspect of his life. We'll never be able to answer it, either. It's so unknowable. But I really think that it tends to weigh on you more if you're having problems with your child. It is just our good fortune that Noah is comfortable in school and with his friends. He's basically doing okay, so we didn't have to search for answers to problems.

When we had minor problems—when Noah was scared of going to school, when he wanted to come home—we didn't think, "Oh, he's crying because he's adopted." We knew he didn't like his teacher; we didn't like the teacher, either. We didn't overthink it. Noah never came home from school saying some kid laughed at him or hit him because he was adopted. To say that there is no trauma resulting from adoption is crazy. But it's all relative.

**Esther:** He's a basically comfortable kid. He's big and he's always been a leader—not in the presidential sense or anything like that. He has a quiet confidence.

**Peter:** Whatever trauma there may be, it is not simply because of the separation from the biological mother. It's what replaces her. A child's life can go from being a little bit traumatic to a lot depending upon what happens next, depending upon how many steps there are to finding a permanent home.

**Esther:** I have strong feelings about infertility treatment. If you want to be a parent, you can. Yes, there is some giving up control when you move to adopt. But I also think that many people who have a hard time accepting the idea of adoption feel that way because they can love only themselves. I wasn't aware of that until we got into this whole adoption process. People frequently come to us asking for advice about adoption. The one thing they always ask is, "Can you love an adopted child?" To me that question means, "Can you love anybody other than yourself?" I wonder if that kind of person is really set up to have a child in the first place.

In the very beginning of our adoption process, people would say such cruel things: "Don't you want to have a real child?" Or "Don't you want your own?" We felt very strongly that we wanted to be parents, but neither Peter nor I had any special attachment to our gene pool. Even if we had had great scholars in our background, we wouldn't have cared about reproducing ourselves. We just wanted to raise a child. The world is filled with millions of children who need homes. When people come to us having spent tens of thousands of dollars on fertility treatments, it makes me a little angry, and a little sad. Because if the goal is to raise a child, you can. Instead of torturing yourself and destroying your relationship, and wreaking havoc on your body, go someplace where there are children who need homes.

**Peter:** Besides, all that fertility stuff eliminates romance from your life. It's very damaging to your relationship. Our limit was about fourteen months. We went to a meeting in this auditorium filled with people who were getting fertility treatment and we decided, "Enough." There was so much tension and pain in that room.

**Esther:** There's little control in the adoption world. For someone like Peter who is very nervous about the unknown, it was hard.

**Peter:** I was scared of any kind of mental health issues. Color, race, or even physical handicaps didn't bother me. Those I could handle. But having a child with a problem that, no matter how much love I gave him or her, I wouldn't be able to fix would be hard for me to live with. Not that I wouldn't have done it. I would have. The only stipulation I actually did make was that I wanted to do a foreign adoption because I was worried about the birth mother changing her mind.

I was never afraid of not bonding. I don't understand that. You bond with pets, with goldfish. I don't mean to be glib, but how could you not bond with a human being? It doesn't mean you're not going to have problems, but you bond. I guess people are afraid of it as a theoretical problem. Maybe it never happens that they can't actually bond once they see the child. Loving is the only part of parenting that's easy.

**Esther:** I really don't think you could say that when it comes to happiness—whatever that means—that biological kids are any happier than adopted kids. We're very aware that no matter what circumstances result in your becoming a family, if it works out it's kind of a miracle. Who knows why? Who knows how even Peter and I came together . . . ?

**Peter:** . . . Harry!

**Esther:** Yeah. Harry.

"*Loving is the only part of parenting that's easy.*"

Kids,
9 to 19

Knowing that they belong

# Caitlin

"I think that you're the one who decides how you're going to get to your parents and who you're going to love."

I have this story about how I came to my family, and I feel it's true. My mom had had a lot of miscarriages before I was born, which worried me. So before I was born, when I was an angel in heaven, I didn't want to be one of those miscarriages—one of the angels it didn't work out for. I decided that the only way to reach my mom was to be born through another woman. I asked God and he said, "Well, give it a try."

When I was in heaven and on the way down to be born, I crashed and hurt my wings—that's why I was born with a curved-in foot. There was this magical monkey that gave me blue sparkly wings to fly with, and I used them to be born. That's how I was brought to the world. It's sort of funny, but I believe that when a person gets pregnant, it's only when the baby is born that the spirit goes into the child.

I think that you're the one who decides how you're going to get to your parents and who you're going to love. When you're adopted, you are with the family with whom you were meant to be.

We're all very strong in my family, but we all pitch in and help each other when we need to. I like the fact that when my parents are making a decision about something in our family, they always ask me my opinion. I like that they help me to handle difficult situations and they give me an honest answer. I'm happy that we talk a lot because I forget things, and also sometimes I don't understand. A lot of my friends don't know how to handle a lot of situations and can't go to their parents for advice.

We have an open adoption, and I think that's very good for me. I've known about my adoption since I was three years old, though my parents told me from the beginning. I know that my birth mom did the right thing and that my parents did a nice thing because instead of being upset that they couldn't have a baby, they decided to adopt, which is really helpful for everybody. I was nervous when I first

Actress Caitlin Wachs, age nine, was adopted at birth in 1989 in an open domestic adoption. Her baby brother, John Whitman, age six months, was also adopted domestically at birth in an open adoption in 1999. Her parents, Patrice and Allen, are interviewed on page 30.

met my birth mother because I didn't know how she was going to react. I thought she either might take me back or something bad was going to happen. We talked, and she gave me a late birthday present. Then I knew that she was just meeting me because she loves me and she wants to know what I'm like.

I'm happy that my parents made the effort to arrange for me to meet her. Before, when I was little, I was embarrassed to talk to my birth mom—I felt shy because I didn't really know her, even though she's kind of like a mother. She was really happy when she first talked to me on the phone and I, well, I don't know, something made me feel weird that she loved me when we hadn't even met yet. But now that I have met her and know what she looks like and have seen her house and her husband, I understand. Now when I say her name, I can picture her. When I talk to her on the phone, I can have a complete conversation with her. I can ask her questions. For example, I have some kind of skin thing on my legs, and it turns out that my birth grandmother had the same problem, so I know what to do for it.

Now I'm not so scared to say I'm adopted. I'm not scared to talk to my birth mom on the phone. I'm not scared at all. I feel that I'm special in that way. I know that everybody in this world has something that's different. When I tell my friends that I'm adopted, they look at me in a weird way. I think they think, "Oh, that's why you're an actress. . . . Your parents made you an actress because they wanted to make you feel good since you're adopted." One of my friends said, "Oh, so you're like Little Orphan Annie." And I said, "No, no, no, that's not like it at all." It's terrible because when that movie came out, it gave everybody this crazy idea that kids are treated in a bad way when they're adopted.

One day, a friend called me up and asked, "Are you adopted?" Of course, I answered yes. But the next day at school I realized that she had told everybody. I told her that this was private information. She started to cry because she thought I was upset with her. I said, "I'm not mad. This is perfect practice for me when I get older. This is easy for me to handle."

Parents are afraid of telling their kids things because of what other kids at school will say about them. But you just have to not take it the wrong way. Kids need to know the truth. Besides, children will always make fun of other children—that's how some of them are. Some kids feel bad when that happens. I know that deep down inside myself there's no difference between you and me. It's not like I'm an animal. When you're adopted, you're still brought into this world, and your mom and dad are your mom and dad. You feel that your birth parents did the right thing. It sort of makes you feel wonderful inside. It makes you feel special.

One girl at school said that if my parents died, I would have to go back to my birth parents. And I said, "No." My parents and I talked about it and they said, "You're going to live with your aunts like you said you wanted to." Well, the whole thing sort of made me feel a little uncomfortable—somebody I don't even know well telling me what's going to happen to me if my parents die. But I just brushed it aside and thought, "If that's what she thinks, that's what she thinks." But I know the truth. I started to think about it and I realized that they're just kids, they can't tell me how I'm going to live my life.

There are a few things that are scary about being adopted. Like I said, the really big thing for me is that sometimes I'm afraid my birth mom might want me back. I know, in a way, that this can't happen, because they simply wouldn't "steal" me back; it's against the law.

Being adopted teaches you about how to handle things, including being adopted. I think I know a lot about the real world. It's sort of weird. I think I'm a strong kind of kid—strong enough to tell people to leave me alone. I don't want to say that I'm a mature person, but mature enough.

I take being adopted as a gift. I don't hide behind it. I deliberately took it upon myself to tell kids because I didn't want other people talking about me. I wanted to be the one who talked about it. I know that some parents are afraid to talk to their kids about it. I think they feel their children might think their parents don't love them as much. A parent might be afraid that a kid would take it the wrong way. But kids get more angry at their parents for not telling them things than for telling them things.

# Josie

## "I know one thing for sure: Your parents are your parents. The people who raise you and take care of you are your parents."

Highly imaginative Josie Adams, age ten, was adopted domestically at birth in 1989. Her sister, Sophie, age five, was also adopted domestically at birth in 1994. Both were adopted in semi-open adoptions by Brooke and Tony, who are interviewed on page 24.

Me and my mom were alone together for about two years. Then my dad came. I believe that my mother and I were brought together by God. We have a lot of fights sometimes, but so does everyone else. We fight about really stupid things like homework and what I'm going to wear in the morning. I can say anything to her. My favorite thing to do is to go to a café and order a *latte* and pretend that we're not mother and daughter but best friends. I'm sure that if we were not mother and daughter, we would be best friends. We would probably want to see each other every day. I love her so much. She's the coolest person. I always talk to her at night about us. After she reads me a book, I ask her questions like, "Were you happy when you got me?" And she says, "What do you think?" She says, "Yes, I wanted you so much." And that makes me so happy.

My birth mother was nineteen when I was born. She was in college so she couldn't raise me. I don't know her. I'm just her birth person. My parents are my parents. When I was four years old or younger, I used to ask my mother where my parents were and how was I born. She would pretend that she didn't hear me because she didn't know how to answer those questions. She didn't know how to say it so that I would understand and not feel bad. She said she went to a psychologist and asked her, "What should I do?" And the psychologist said, "Just tell her the truth." After that, my mom answered me and said, "Your birth mom and dad are from Omaha, Nebraska." I never asked again. I didn't need to know any more; her answer was good enough.

My mom says that when I'm around eighteen, I could meet my birth mother. We have pictures of her on our wall, which I like to look at. We also send her pictures every Christmas. She doesn't write back or say anything. One time she wrote a letter

and said, "My daughter is so beautiful." And I noticed that she said "my daughter." This made me nervous. I thought, "She still considers that I'm hers. I'm legally my parents', but it's just kind of scary to think that if there wasn't a law, birth parents could come and say, 'I want my child back.' I know one thing for sure: Your parents are your parents. The people who raise you and take care of you are your parents.

When my dad came, at first I didn't feel comfortable calling him Dad. I was so used to just having my mom. But then when I was three years old, I once tried it out, and I called him Dad. I giggled. I felt more attached to him, and forever. I was really happy when my mom and dad got married. Then Sophie came. I didn't really like it that much. I thought I lost some attention. I asked my mother the other day, "Would you be happy without Sophie?" She said, "No, because having Sophie makes me feel closer to you. With Sophie we have a more complete family, and I wanted you to have that."

At the beginning of the school year, some kids teased me and said, "You're adopted." And I said, "Yeah, who cares?" Then they said, "Well, you're adopted, so who's your real mom?" "My parents are my real parents," I told them. "My parents signed a contract, and that makes them my real parents. I love them." Sometimes kids tease other kids just because they're unhappy themselves. One day this boy came up to me and teased me, saying, "You're adopted," and I said, "That's okay. It's really cool." Then he teased me about being older than him. It didn't matter what it was, he just wanted to tease me.

I recently said to one of my close friends who sometimes acts weird around me, "You know, it's okay being adopted. You don't have to treat me differently. You can ask me about it." And she sighed and said, "Oh, thank goodness!"

I feel really special being adopted. Sometimes kids who were not adopted act like they're better than you are. But I stand tall. At school we do this thing every week where we sit in a circle and talk about kids being nasty to each other. I brought up being adopted. And I told everyone that it's okay to be adopted. Everybody was born. It's all the same. Even if you were born from one person and have a different set of parents, you still have your parents. You're still a kid like everyone else.

I think kids have to learn more about how to care about other people's feelings. Adopted kids often have more sensitivity to kids who are different. One day me and my friend were the last people at lunch, and we were talking about things. I said, "I'm adopted and I feel like I know how to handle things." And my friend said, "Yes, you're very mature. And I also think you're very brave because you can stand up to those mean people." People who act higher than you are probably really jealous of you.

I love my parents, I love my sister, but sometimes we get into fights. Sophie is so strong. When my parents go upstairs Sophie scares me so much because she plays so rough. She gets upset sometimes and says things like my mom doesn't give her candy. Then she'll say to my mom, "My real mom is better than you. I don't like you. I'm going home to my real mom." But then right after that she'll say, "Oh, I love you, Mom. I hate my real mom." I say to her, "Make up your mind."

I have a lot of days that I really like. But one of the best days was my tenth birthday. I had a dance party. All my best friends came, which was so great. I also had a great day when we went to Wisconsin and visited all my relatives. I have a lot of relatives—like twenty. I loved being with my family.

On that same day I watched the movie *My Fair Lady.* A few weeks later, when we were back in Los Angeles, we rented *Breakfast at Tiffany's.* These are my two absolutely favorite movies. When I watch *Breakfast at Tiffany's,* I always fantasize that I'm Audrey Hepburn. She's my favorite actress—except for my mom.

If I could talk to my birth mom, I would ask her why she had me at her age. I'd tell her that I'm glad that she brought me to my parents. When I told this to people in my class, everybody was shocked. They thought, "How horrible." I guess they just don't understand. I think I have the best life anybody could have.

*"I'm sure that if we were not mother and daughter, we would be best friends."*

# Sevi

## "I didn't figure out I was adopted until I was six or seven. My parents told me much earlier, but I didn't know what it meant."

I don't think that if I was born into my family, it would be any different from being adopted. People ask me if I was adopted since I look different from my family. And then I tell them I'm adopted. They say okay; they don't think it's a big deal. I think the same way. There are a few kids in our grade, however, who think they're better than me because I'm adopted. But it's not just me they think they're better than, it's everybody. They think they're so cool. But they're not. It bothers my sister, Madden, but it doesn't bother me at all. I feel that I'm like every other kid. I like to skateboard and swim, I Rollerblade, and I bike. I hike a lot and I love camping and living in the woods.

I've never felt that being adopted makes me feel far away from my parents. I know I can always ask them about being adopted. They don't make me worry that it might hurt their feelings. And I've wondered a little bit about my birth parents—who they are, what they look like—but I don't think about it that much. If I could meet them, I do have a few questions I'd like to ask. I'd want to know if they went to college. I heard that my birth mom was too young to take care of me and so she had to find a home for me. Sometimes I wonder what she does for a living. If I could find out, I would want to. My dad says he might take me to Colombia one day and look her up. But it's not always on my mind.

Some of my friends think that being adopted means that your biological parents didn't like you. I don't believe that. You hadn't even said anything yet, maybe you just cried. Why would anybody give you up because of that?

# Madden

"I really don't know who I look like, and I would like to know. I've never seen a picture of my birth mom or dad. I'd like to know how I got red hair and freckles."

Red-haired L.A. girl Madden Foreman, age nine, was adopted at four months in 1990 from Colombia. Her brother, Sevi, age eleven, also born in Colombia, was adopted at three months in 1988. His interview appears on page 77, and their parents' interview appears on page 21.

People think that if you're adopted you're like Little Orphan Annie. It's so silly. Being adopted is really not much different from being born from your mother. Not everybody in my school knows I'm adopted. I don't know many other kids who were adopted. Except for my friend Josie Adams and my brother, I'm the only person I know who was adopted.

I do think a lot about being adopted. When I was little, I just wished that I could suck on my mom's breast. I keep on thinking about that. I also wish that my parents would have been there the day I was born. When you're adopted, the birth parents are the people who see you first. The parents that adopt you don't see what you look like when you're just born. Maybe some people do in a different situation, but I was adopted when I was four months old. My brother was adopted when he was three months old. My parents had to wait an extra month for me because the people who worked at the adoption place couldn't let them take me right away.

I also wonder if my parents would have adopted me if I was four years old. I think about how I would look if I was born from my mom's belly. Would I kind of look the way I do even though my mom doesn't look like me?

My parents and I talk about visiting Colombia someday. I try to remember it in my dreams. But after a couple of years, your memories just go away because you're with your parents. If we do go to Colombia, we're going to try to see if I can meet my birth mother. My parents explained that she was too young, and I pretty much understood that. If I could, I'd ask her if she had been a little older, would she have kept me.

*"My parents and I talk about visiting Colombia someday.*
*I try to remember it in my dreams. But after a couple of years, your*
*memories just go away because you're with your parents."*

I really don't know who I look like, and would like to know. I've never seen a picture of my birth mom or dad. I'd like to know how I got red hair and freckles. Everybody asks me, "Why don't you and your brother look anything alike?" And I say because we're adopted. They're really amazed by that.

When I was in third grade, I wrote this paper about adoption. I asked my teacher if anybody in my class was adopted. The teacher said I was the only one. I felt kind of weird that there was no one else in my class or in the school. They don't really tell you about other kids. I think it would be really good for adopted kids to know who the other adopted kids are around them.

Sevi's my older brother, and I love him, but we do fight all the time. We're so different. We never tease each other about the same thing. For example, he teases me about having freckles. I tease him about the fact that he is so much lighter-skinned than me because he was born in the city and I was born in the mountains. I have Indian blood, which is okay. That's just the way it is. Sometimes when we fight we later forgive each other. I often wish I had a sister. Or I wish I was a twin. Me and my best friend, Josie Adams, who was adopted, are like sisters. She wants to look like me and I want to look like her.

Being adopted makes me feel really special. I feel like my mom and dad picked me; they didn't pick anybody else. And they make me feel good about adoption. I can talk to them about anything. When I was younger, I was a little nervous about talking to my parents, about asking them questions about my adoption. Finally, I just asked my mom a lot of questions. We talked about it and it was really okay.

# Jared

"I think everybody should understand what adoption is, because if they have the wrong ideas and a chance comes for them to adopt and raise a child, they're not going to take it because they'll be scared of what they don't know."

Hockey-playing Jared Goldberg, age fourteen, was domestically adopted at birth in 1985 in a closed adoption. His sisters Whitney, age ten and a half, born in 1987, and Kayla, age eight and a half, born in 1990, are biological to his parents, Mitchell and Joann, who are interviewed on page 55.

I'm starting high school, which is three miles out in the middle of nowhere. I'm excited because most of my friends are coming with me, but I'm also a little nervous and sad about leaving some of my friends behind. I guess I'm going from being a kid to starting to be an adult. I was thinking that my life is going by so fast.

I think adopted kids might have a little bit of a harder time with all this change and leaving their families because they might feel a little different. They might feel like the odd one out among their friends. Some kids have a problem with self-esteem and they can't talk about it, but I'm not embarrassed about it. Whenever the subject comes up, I say I'm adopted. It's no big deal. I can talk about it, but I don't announce it. Most of my friends know I'm adopted. I tell them all about it. Most of the time they forget. I don't really think about it that often. I don't really feel that being adopted is much different. I didn't come from Mars. You still came out of someone's stomach, and we all come out equal.

I never feel confused about who I am because I'm adopted. My parents told me everything, and I know all I need to know about it. I would never keep my adoption a secret. And when I'm old enough and married, I would never keep it a secret from my wife and kids. Being adopted is just one part of me.

I guess adoption can be kind of a challenge. It's like when I started playing hockey, I wasn't that great at it. But I've practiced a lot, and now I'm pretty good. I was

embarrassed at first by the other kids who were better than me because they were at it much longer. I didn't give up because I liked playing a lot. I wanted to improve. So I learned. I just faced the challenge.

One girl in my class once asked me, "Well, do you know your biological parents?" And I said, "No." And she said, "Oh, that's so sad." "It's not sad," I said. "I have my parents and I live here." Other kids in school just don't understand what it feels like to be adopted. I explain some things to them, and I also tell them, "I don't want to ruin anything or hurt my parents by wondering too much about my birth parents. I'm not that interested, and I don't want to take that risk. I like it here." Even if my parents told me it wouldn't hurt them and they don't care, I still feel that I don't need to know more. I don't need to go out searching. My life's right here. I don't need to find another life. I would feel so weird just talking to my parents about it. I'd have it in the back of my mind that they'd think I was telling them, "You weren't enough." If my mom says it would make her wonder, "Did I do anything wrong?" it would make me hesitate. I wouldn't want to hurt her.

My parents have always told me about how and where I was born. They got a call just after I was born. It was my dad's birthday, so I was his birthday present. Our birthdays are three days apart. My mom called her mother and told her that she got me, but she hadn't told her if I was a boy or a girl. Then they called back and asked. They were so happy. They sent flowers.

My mom and dad did tell me that my biological father was really tall, and so I'm going to be tall when I grow up. And my biological mother had brown hair and brown eyes, and so do I. I always knew I had those biological traits in common with them. I don't know how old they were when I was born. I know that they were religious and they wanted me to go to a good Jewish home.

I think for birth parents to decide to find a home for their kid is really hard. But it's doing a good thing. I think it's great that they don't put their child in an orphanage or get an abortion. It gives the child a good life. It's also good that birth parents make the decision right away. This gives kids a chance to get close to their parents when they're young, instead of waiting until they're five or six, when it gets harder to get close. I'm very grateful to my birth mom. I think she gave me to my parents out of love.

Do I feel more mature, more sensitive being an adopted kid? No, I didn't feel like I had to grow up faster than anybody else. I'm not saying I'm not sensitive, but I don't think it comes from being adopted. I don't think I'm any different from anyone else. My parents told me I was adopted and I said, "That's good, that's great. You're my parents. Let's move on with it."

I can imagine some people being closed-minded to the subject of adoption because they don't understand it. I think everybody should understand what adoption is about, because if they don't and a chance comes for them to adopt and raise a child, they're not going to take it because they'll be scared of what they don't know.

It feels great to grow up in this family. I have everything I need. I love my mom and I love my dad, and I love my sisters.

# Sarah

"I feel happy to be where I am. I am the daughter of my mom and dad. You grow into your mom, and she grows into you."

Horseback-riding, ice-skating, soccer-playing Sarah Kinn, age ten, was adopted domestically at birth in 1989 in a semi-open adoption. Her parents, Mark and Hannah, are interviewed on page 48.

Some kids feel that being adopted is the same as being born to your parents, and some kids feel that it's different. To me, it's the same thing, only a little bit different: You're not exactly from your mom. You're from another mom.

It's surprising how many kids in my school are adopted. Sometimes it comes up, but mostly we just forget. We're all just the same old people. We have the same old fun. We have the same old arm—which some people can or cannot throw a ball with. And we play the same old dodge ball. We live in the same old houses. We're just people. We just came to our families differently.

I think adoption is actually really great. If you go to a very poor country, you'll see some kids walking around in very bad shape without shoes or clothes. But other kids are brought to orphanages and can get adopted by a family, which is good. I don't think that I would have been on the streets. In this country, there are lots of parents who can't have kids and really want kids. It's different here.

Probably life would be a lot different growing up with somebody else. Sometimes you enjoy your life as an adoptee better than your life with a birth mom. Some birth moms are very young, or don't want kids, or just aren't ready for them. Whether they give you up out of love or rejection depends. In some cases, like if you're a supermodel and you don't want to have a kid, it's rejection. You wouldn't have a second thought about it. But if you love the baby, you would go through a lot of trouble deciding where the baby would go. It's all a matter of the work you put into it. It's like if you adopt a dog but you don't think twice about it, you really don't care about the dog. You just say, "I want a dog and I'm just going to get one." If you want a dog really really badly, you read a lot of books and think about it a lot. You go out of your way. Before I got my dog, I read lots and lots of books about him.

I think it's really great to have a birth mom like that, someone who has thought about what she was going to do. It might have been hard for my birth mom to keep me, and she thought it would be hard for me to be with her. I'm really glad that she gave me to my parents. I like where I ended up. I feel wanted by my parents. I was born on December 17, 1989, and my mom and dad came to get me on December 19. I was two days old, a very good age to adopt a child. It's better to adopt a child at two days than at two years, when the child has some memories.

I feel happy to be where I am. I am the daughter of my mom and dad. You grow into your mom, and she grows into you. I am also very close to my aunt Linda and aunt Gail [pictured here]. My dad loves to horseback-ride. My mom hates to—she thinks she'll fall off the horse in five minutes. My father likes jazz, hip-hop, opera, and all kinds of music. My family has something in common all around. Me and my mom like painting. My mom and dad like classical music. Me and my dad like jazz. We all like the water—which has to be lukewarm for my mom to get in. But me and my dad just go Boogieboarding all over the place. The big thing is we all like to read and to exercise. It's just like this thing that we have.

I do feel wanted by my birth mom. I don't feel rejected by her. I think she was too young for a kid. But even though she may have wanted me really badly, she had to give me up. It's like having to say, "I can't get this dog even if I want to. I just can't do this." You just have to accept that you can't do anything about it. A birth mother might think, "If I try to keep the baby, even though it won't be good for the baby, it might hurt him more." Then she should just let him go. This birth mom—even if she feels a lot of pain—knows what's best for the kid. I feel that my birth mom loved me, but she couldn't take care of me and wanted to find a good place for me. She found my parents, and I want to stick with them.

Later on, say at eighteen, some kids go off and find their birth mom to say hello to her. I would want to meet my birth mom, but I want to know a lot of things about her before I make that decision. First, I want to speak to my mom about what my birth mom was like when she met her. I want to know how old she was when I was born. I want to know what her favorite things to do were, to see if we have things in common. I want to know what she looked like, where she lived, and what her last name was. I want to know how she felt when she gave me up. I saw a commercial on television about a company that can help you find anybody. I want to put my birth mom's name up on the Internet and check it out. I want to know if she is alive and, if not, who her relatives are. I do ask my parents questions about my birth mom, but I just ask them little questions like what her name was—not her last name or anything, I don't want to know that right now. It's not exactly my first choice to know. I don't think it would hurt my mommy's or my daddy's feelings if I wanted to find my birth mom.

I would be afraid to meet my birth mom, and I might even have second thoughts. But if I did meet her, I'd be really sad if we didn't have anything in common, and if she might not like me. I would feel really really sad to know that we're connected, and that she likes me a lot, and then find out she likes alcohol and drugs—and I don't. I'd feel really bad to come such a long way and find out that she's not the one that I expected. But I would think that she would like me, and that we would have things in common like shopping and horseback riding. She would live some place that I would like and she would like the place that I live. I would think that we could be friends or something. Though it would be a little weird to be friends with your birth mom.

Sometimes I think my parents and other people try to talk to me about adoption more than I want to. But that depends on what they ask me. Sometimes people ask, "What does it feel like?" and I get sick of them asking that. I like other things like horseback riding.

Some kids think that being adopted makes them different, but I think it's your choice to feel different. It's also your choice to go out and find your birth mom; if you want to find your birth mom, you should follow your dreams. Just find what you want to do. Some kids may say they don't want to find their birth mom, but I think they're curious and they don't want to admit it. They want to forget about it. I think that's a very bad thing. I think you should follow your dreams. Sometimes you get too old to do things you want to do. So you should just always chase your dreams, and never let them go. I think I want to find my birth mom some day . . . but it depends. It depends on a little bit of this, and a little bit of that. . . . *Oy vey,* I don't exactly know.

# Kids
# Grown Up

Reflecting on their contentments and on their challenges

# Jessie

"If I had anything to say to adopted kids—words that I would have wanted to hear myself—I would say, 'Always know that you were wanted.' That's a big issue for adopted kids."

A history major at the George Washington University, Jessie Gordon, age twenty, was adopted domestically in a closed adoption in 1980, when she was ten weeks old, by Barry and Eileen Gordon. At the age of seventeen, she met her birth mother. Her sister, Nora, age nineteen, is biological to their parents.

All my life I've asked myself, "Why am I so lucky?" My parents are so wonderful and they raised me so well. I couldn't have asked for more. I know the life I would have had had I not been adopted. Does that mean that there was always this special place meant for me? I was talking with a friend last week, and he asked, "How would your life have been if you hadn't grown up with your family in Shaker Heights?" It's so difficult for me to answer that question because, unlike a biological kid, it really almost didn't happen.

The first time I realized that there was something different about my life was in kindergarten. I was in the school bathroom and my friends were teasing me saying how weird it was that I didn't know who my mother was. I remember that afternoon so explicitly. I stood on the top of the stairway in my house crying hysterically because I didn't want to be so different. My mom called up to me and we talked. "We chose you," she said. "We saw you and we loved you so much that we wanted you to be ours. Other kids don't have that feeling of being special; they weren't chosen." My parents always said that, and it always made me feel good. How you interpret that, however, when you're younger is very different from what you know when you're older. You know you weren't exactly chosen. Still, it was very positive feedback at a time when I most needed it.

Things changed after that incident; being adopted was no longer negative. I began to view being a little different as a positive thing. When I was younger, just

knowing that other kids were adopted also made me feel grounded. I liked reading *How It Feels to Be Adopted.* Reading books about other kids really helped.

When I was fifteen I was in therapy for a number of problems both related and unrelated to adoption. I also knew I wanted to search for my birth mother. There was always an empty part of me. I knew I was part of a triad: me, my parents, and my birth parents. I wanted to be connected to them all. I wanted to know who I looked like. Who created me? Where did I come from? Where would I be if I hadn't been adopted? The starting point is "Who do I look like?" It links you up with your history. I think even if all you have is a picture of your biological mother, it's important to see that she does exist. She isn't just someone in your imagination. My therapist was an adoption specialist who worked with birth mothers, parents, kids, everyone connected to adoption. She told me I was unique in wanting to search at such an early age. She warned me that I would have to go through a lot of emotional upheaveal, that "even adults have a hard time with it." But I knew I had to try.

It took two years. I was seventeen when I found my birth mother. I met her on Mother's Day in 1997. I met my birth father in my senior year of high school six months later. It was a very different experience. My birth mother is living on very thin means. Though I'm glad I found her, we do have a few problems with each other.

She has become a little dependent on me to be there for her family, and I do feel some pressure from her, which isn't fair. I have big issues with how much she places herself in my life. I've told my birth mom things about her behavior that disturb me. She gives me the biggest guilt trips about not calling her kids and about not calling her enough, particularly when I'm home for school breaks. I tell her I'm going to call and then I don't. Finally, I just told her, "I rarely get to be with my parents anymore. I just don't have the time to call." I hate to have to turn people away. She gave me the gift of life and gave me the opportunity to live my life in a wonderful way. And I do appreciate it. But this isn't fair.

When you think about your birth parents before you find them, you fantasize a lot: "What if they're dead? What if they're rich? What if they don't want to see me? What if they're famous?" But I never ever thought that I would have to deal with any problems. My mom told me I used to have dreams about my birth mother. When I was older, I think I wanted *her* to find *me.* But when I was young, I was always afraid that she would kidnap me. Oddly enough, my parents did hear from a mutual friend of my biological aunt—through whom my parents found me—that when I was four years old my birth mother got back together with my birth father and they decided they were going to find me. But they broke up again before that ever happened.

*"I needed to know my birth parents to be who I am today."*

*"One of the good things that's come with knowing my birth mother*

*is that I no longer feel the pang of being given up."*

Though I didn't meet with my birth mother until I was seventeen, I do think it would have been good for me to meet her when I was very young, just to see this flesh-and-blood person who cared enough to see the child she gave up. However, I'm not necessarily in favor of a total open adoption where the birth mother is involved in the child's life on a regular basis. I think that would be so confusing for a young child because of all the conflicting ties.

There was this possibility of inviting my birth mom to my senior high school ballet performance, but my parents weren't ready to meet her. I can't imagine how my mother would have felt. My parents and my birth mother still haven't met. I don't know where my birth mother fits in. I'm confused. My parents were always so open about the adoption, and about my wanting to search. Once the search became a reality, it was a little harder on all of us.

One of the good things that's come with knowing my birth mother is that I no longer feel the pang of being given up. I hated her for giving me up. During that two-year process of reunion, I remember just crying all the time, saying, "I wish she had never given me up because I wouldn't have had to go through all this emotional stress." But now that I know where I came from, it's different.

My birth father, by contrast, had some problems in his early years, but he got married and became a born-again Christian. When we met, he told me that no one in his family knows about me and that his wife was about to have their first child. He couldn't find it in himself to tell her. I said, "That's just fine. I just wanted to meet you." He said, "If you are ever in any trouble, if you ever need me, if you ever get sick and need money or anything, call me. I'll be there. But I can't be involved in any relationship." I said, "That's fine." I don't think I could have dealt with any more. I just needed to know my birth parents to be who I am today.

My mom and I have had some rough times, but it's gotten so much better since I met my birth parents and went away to college. I eventually realized that I resented the fact that my mother was not my birth mother. I blamed her for the fact that I didn't come from her. It's ironic to use the word *blame* because she mattered to me, and I was blaming her because she mattered. We're very much alike, and we butt heads a lot. I always used to say things like, "I am the boss of myself." I was very disrespectful to her. I did a lot of rebellious things. I took her credit cards. I took the car out when I was under age and got into a little trouble. I stole money from them. I didn't do drugs or anything like that. I just did things to test them. It was like I was

asking, "If I was mean to you, if I took your money, if I lied to you, would you still love me, or are you going to leave me?" They realized what was going on and reassured me that they would never, ever leave me no matter how bad things got. This was happening when I was fifteen or sixteen. I was, as they say, acting out. But even when we fought, I'd never use the word *hate;* I'd never say, "I wish you weren't my parents." My sister could say terrible things about my parents; I did too, but I was more careful. Even when I was young I never said, "I wish you hadn't adopted me."

Meeting my birth mother made me more forgiving. I couldn't have asked for more support from my parents. I understood how much my parents loved and cared for me. I can picture both my parents giving their lives for me. I saw my mother cry over my connecting with my birth mother, but she let me go. She knew I had to do this to complete myself as a person.

I really understood the issues that come up around being adopted when I was in therapy. The first one is big-time insecurity with relationships—not just with my parents, but in high school with boyfriends. I would break up with wonderful guys in three weeks out of fear that they would leave me first.

Another huge issue for me was choosing my religion. Both my adoptive and my birth moms are Catholics. My father is Jewish. They let me and my sister choose our faith. We both chose to be Jewish. I feel Jewish. My rabbi wrote a book about the origins of religious feelings and concluded that religion comes from within the person, not with birth. I was mentioned in the same chapter of the book as Elie Wiesel, which was an honor. Judaism is very alive in my family, though we celebrate both Christian and Jewish holidays.

I was talking to my friend recently about adoption and he said, "You use adoption too much. You use it to justify too many things. You use it as an explanation for everything." Maybe he was right. I may use it to my advantage sometimes.

If I had anything to say to adopted kids—words that I would have wanted to hear myself—I would say, "Always know that you were wanted." That's a big issue for adopted kids. They think, "Nobody wanted me. That's why I don't have a birth mother." Adopted kids need to know that they were wanted, that their birth parents loved them so much and knew they couldn't give them the life they wanted them to have, and that it was the hardest thing for their birth mothers to give them up. I didn't know that for too long.

*"Much of my anger went away after I met my birth mother.*

*It made me more forgiving."*

# Peter

## "Adoption is not something to get over. It's part of who I am."

Peter Savasta, age twenty-four, was born in Seoul, South Korea, and adopted at five months in 1976 by Mary and Lenny Savasta. His sister, Suzanne, age thirty-one, and brother, Anthony, age thirty-four, are both biological to their parents. Peter is vice president of Also Known As, Inc., an association of adult Korean adoptees.

I grew up in Queens—a bastion of Italian-American life—where I now live near my parents and my sister. But I was born in Seoul, South Korea. I came to be adopted by my parents when they realized they couldn't have any more children because of a conflict in blood types. It was 1975 and Vietnam was just evacuating Saigon. My parents were very affected by the airlift of orphans that crashed. When my mother contacted the New York Foundling Center to see if any of those children had survived, they said that those who had survived all had families waiting for them. But the social worker told her that there were also children in Korea who didn't have homes. And my mother said, "I don't care where they're from. If there are children who don't have homes, I want to give them one. I just want a child." She always says to me, "I know that God wanted us to meet. That you were destined for me."

My mother told me that she felt that the love for me and from me are no different than with my brother and sister. "I already have children, and I know that it doesn't matter what you call that affinity. In the end, we're family."

Finding my way through this background—Korean-Italian-American adoptee—has been like swinging on a pendulum. At different stages in my life the pendulum has swung from my identification with my Italian-American roots over to my Korean birth and then back again. When I was young, I went through a long stage during which being adopted was a great thing to me. Being Korean was never an issue with my good friends. But sometimes, other kids would give me a hard time. I remember coming home from school one day when I was six and asking my mother, "What does *chink* mean?" She said, "The kids who call you that are envious. They say it because you stand out, because you're special. If they felt better about themselves they wouldn't bother with that."

After this incident, my mother talked to my teacher, who suggested that I should have come to her first; that had I done so, she would have talked to the other kids and stood up for me. "Don't do that," my mother responded, "because he's going to have to deal with this for the rest of his life. As hard as this sounds, he's going to have to know how to defend himself." She was right.

Having to learn about issues of racism at the age of six was often difficult. I remember some of the kids insisted that I had to look like my parents if I was going to call them my parents. They couldn't comprehend that relationships not based on blood could be real. Sometimes I dealt with these remarks sarcastically, not so nobly. I sort of reveled in their ignorance. I know that I was being defensive. I'd say, "Ah, no, they're just baby-sitting me." When I got frustrated, sometimes I would just tell wild stories to

people. I told one story when I was studying biology and learning about regressive genes—I told people that my parents were Italian and I was born to them, but since one of my ancestors, who was in the trade envoys in Asia, took an Asian wife, once in every generation that whole regressive gene thing takes over and a completely Asian child is born. And that explains me. People would say, "Wow!" Later I'd think, "That's not very nice," and I would get real and tell them, "No, seriously, I'm adopted."

I didn't want to always have to explain myself, but I went through life thinking I had to. Being able to choose privacy when you want to is crucial to an adopted child, who may sometimes feel his life is an open book. It's not always uncomfortable to answer those questions. But I want it to be my choice. The only time I really don't have a choice about explaining

myself is when I pay with my credit card because my name doesn't match my face. That's a pain.

Being adopted and being a little different was cool until I turned thirteen. Then I had the whole teenage identity crisis, which can be—and was—amplified by adoption. Often, too, at this stage, being adopted is used as an explanation for a multitude of problems that have little to do with it. It's difficult to separate issues of adolescence from issues of adoption. Adolescence is the time when the meaning of things, including adoption, starts to change. And it certainly did for me. "Given up for adoption" turned into feelings of being abandoned by my biological mother. But I don't feel it that strongly anymore. Knowing the reality of what happened when I was born has replaced that. And meeting another birth mother for the first time also had a big impact on me. Even though she was Caucasian, I felt some identification with her because her son would have been my age. Her issues of separation and guilt and grief were powerful. It made me think about my birth parents and their courage in being able to walk away and not know what happened to me. I started wishing I could meet my birth mother and thank her and tell her I'm okay and how much I respect her. She made sure to take care of herself even though she was so poor, and in taking care of herself she took care of me. Now that I have seen that process of grieving in another birth mother, I know I was loved.

Still, I definitely had to get over the "what was wrong with me?" sense of myself that often comes with being adopted. I went through that whole anxiety that something must have been bad in me for my birth mother to have given me up. Then, to make things harder, I felt that I had to live up to the expectations of my adoptive parents because they wanted and loved me so much. I didn't want to disappoint them. I didn't want to show anyone any part of me that was unacceptable.

When I was younger and then when I was a teenager, there were times when I saw myself as an American more than anything else. I didn't even consider myself Asian. I went to the Bronx High School of Science,

*"It's difficult to separate issues of adolescence from issues of adoption."*

which had a very diverse population. There were some Asian students, but I wasn't strongly identified with them. Most of my friends were Jewish. But I also felt like I was living two different lives. When I was at home with my parents, I was just me. At school, I was just me. But when I looked into a mirror, I'd stop suddenly and say to myself, "Oh, right, I *am* Asian."

But soon the pendulum started swinging toward things Korean. I began noticing more hate crimes against Asians, and I realized that no matter who I was, people were going to identify me from the outside, because that's what they generally do. Then, during the L.A. riots in 1992, I watched the largest community of Korean Americans living in the United States burning down. That's when it really got to me that as much as I assert myself as a person of a multicultural background, my race is going to be the first perception people are going to have of me. I began to think, "I'm Korean, and I have to acknowledge that."

By the time I left high school and went to college in upstate New York, the pendulum just swung all the way over to Korea. I got involved in the Korean-American community through the church. It was a rude and difficult awakening. Coming from New York and a school that was very diverse to an environment that was very homogeneous, very WASPy, was hard. And it was then that I had my first frightening experience with overt racism. One day I came back from class and found one of my architecture projects destroyed. Things were stolen from my room. It was like living through a freshman hazing, a rite of passage, but much worse.

Participating in the Korean-American church opened up my understanding. I learned more about the culture and I also got "the old-time religion." I got a bit more radical. Little by little I grew distant from my Italian culture. My associations were mainly with Koreans and Asians, and I shifted away from mainstream American culture. At one point everyone was calling me by my Korean name, which at first I thought was great. But then I realized that I really didn't feel comfortable answering to that name. I asked people to call me Peter, and many of them said, "But you're Korean and you should have a Korean name." "But I'm also adopted," I told them, "and I have this whole other side of me. My face shows I'm Korean, but it doesn't show everything else; that's why I'm keeping my name. 'Peter Savasta' is important to me." Once again, the pendulum swung, now the other way, toward Queens.

The pendulum is finally losing its momentum altogether and coming to a place of rest. If I can't find the precise words to define who I am, that's okay. In aspects of culture and ethnicity, we assume that we all have to be put into one category or another. But if you or I look at an entire life, I'd have to say, "Well, I'm Korean, but I'm also Italian American, I'm a son, but I'm also an uncle, and so on." Adoption is not something to get over. It's part of who I am.

For many years I tried not to show my parents all the swings of the pendulum. At one point I was very distant because I didn't want to hurt them with all I was going through. And I thought if I was very distant, it would hurt them less. But the message I got from my parents was always "You can't get rid of us so easily."

I've always had close relationships with my parents and my siblings. I sometimes think my brother and sister thought my parents overcompensated with me; that they may have spoiled me in some way. Whether they felt that that was a result of my being so much younger than them or because I was adopted, I'm not sure. There may be a little resentment, but we do get along and love each other very much.

When I started my search process, the big thing for me was moving back into my past. Even though I knew my parents were behind me and my father said, "We'll help you," I always felt that that was just something that parents say. Recently we talked and I said, "I can't go ahead with this search if I know it's going to hurt you." And my dad said, "You know, Peter, we were expecting this. This is another part of your life. We would never try to hold this back from you." And then he said something that really took my breath away. He said, "If we couldn't handle this, we wouldn't have adopted you."

The one thing my parents do worry about in regard to my finding my birth mother is the possibility that when I meet her, she might reject me. They fear that I would be so disappointed and crushed. I had to assure them that it would be okay. You can't imagine the scenarios I came up with as a child about my birth parents. I imagined them as nobility. I imagined my mother as a prostitute. I imagined myself as the product of a rape. I think if anything negative happened in that reunion, yes, I would be hurt, but I wouldn't be shocked because I'm not going expecting a simple, happy encounter.

Over time, I've found that I've had to create a special space for myself, a place where all the different aspects of my personality would be validated. I've found this in many corners of my life but particularly in my involvement with a group of other adoptees in the organization of which I am currently vice president called Also Known As, Inc., which is an association of adult Korean adoptees.

Prospective parents of international adoptees often ask me, "How much cultural background should I give my child? And my answer is, "Until they reject it." For kids, it's great to participate in cultural events, but what they really want is to go out and play with their friends. They want and need to fit in. Make their background available but don't push it on them. And don't discount the fact that your culture is as important to them as any other. Culture is learned; it's a gift that's passed on from generation to generation. Connections are not automatic, they have to be worked at.

In the end I think I had to grow up in order to take whatever aspect of Korean culture I cared about for myself. My ownership of it is what matters. I don't know how it would have worked if my parents had learned Korean and tried to pass it on to me; it would have felt secondhand. It's difficult to know what to do. Every family is different.

# Jaime

## "I don't picture myself as being saved by my parents. I feel as grateful that my parents adopted me as they do."

Adoption lawyer Jaime Greenberg, age twenty-six, was two months old when he was adopted from Colombia in 1973 by Barbara and Joel, who are interviewed on page 35. Today, Jaime is a partner in his family's adoption law firm. His older brother, Charles, age thirty-two, and sister, Kim, age twenty-eight, are biological to their parents. (His fiancée, Janice, is pictured with him.)

I grew up under the spotlight of adoption. My parents were adoption lawyers, and because of that I was making speeches in front of fifteen hundred people when I was twelve. For twenty-six years, adoption has been the centerpiece of my life. Now that I've become an attorney and have joined my parents' adoption law practice, it will continue to be central to my life. Being the "poster" child for adoption put me on a pedestal, and I soaked up and enjoyed every second of it. I was interviewed by a newspaper reporter who wrote, "This is a great way to make a family." But when adoption set me apart from my family, whether innocently or maliciously, that's when it hurt.

The first time I realized I was adopted I was around five or six. I got into a fight with a little boy on my front lawn when he said, "You're not your parents' son. You don't look like them." I began thinking, "Maybe I'm adopted." I went into the house and talked to my mom, and she explained everything to me. I know my parents must have told me before, but it didn't register until someone my own age threw it in my face.

I love my family. I've always had a wonderful relationship with my brother, Charles, and my sister, Kim, who are older and biological to my parents. Growing up, my sister gave me a blanket of security; she dealt with anyone who might look at me sideways. She loved to goad people. Once, while I was helping her at the bakery where she was working, someone asked about me. "He's my brother," she said. The person was mindless enough to say, "Well, you don't look alike. One of you must be adopted." She looked him straight in the eye, and without missing a beat, she said, "That's me!"

I grew up in an area of Long Island that was predominantly middle- and upper-middle-class, hardworking Catholics and Christians. I was one of only two Jewish kids in the school, and there were no Hispanics. Luckily, it was a great community. Very tolerant. I never felt awkward or odd in school. I knew I was Colombian and felt some tie to the country, but I never dug deeply into my heritage. In fourth grade I drew a big map of Colombia, and was very pleased with it. The following year I drew a map of Israel. My life was a blend of the two.

Many adoptive parents of international children worry about how much cultural education they should give them. Parents often ask me if my family had "taco night." In other words: Do you teach your adopted Chinese daughter how to use chopsticks when she's two years old? Do you serve tacos to your Mexican boy? I'd always answer, "To each his own." There is definitely no set of rules on how to raise your children, but I wouldn't push the culture on them. Eventually, they're going to make their own choices. My parents never imposed Colombian culture on me. I grew up with matzoh balls and gefilte fish. If I had to identify myself culturally, I'd say I'm a Long Island Jewish Colombian. Long Island being first, because that was the culture I was most familiar and comfortable with.

I'm happy I was adopted. I've often wondered about what my life would have been like if I'd grown up in Colombia. Maybe I would have been the next great soccer star on the Colombian national team. My friends joke around all the time, saying, "Oh, you'd be running around in the streets." I never think that way, but I guess it could have happened. That's something I don't like to think about—how bad it could have been. You never know.

I always wanted to know about my biological parents' physical characteristics. I wanted to see pictures. I wanted to know their medical history, too. I was one of the shortest kids in elementary school. When everyone else was getting taller, and I could see that because their father or mother was tall that they were going to be very tall, I didn't have any references. On the flip side, I kind of had an advantage. I was the only Hispanic soccer player at Skidmore. Everyone assumed that I would be fantastic and accepted me immediately.

Last year my mother and I went back to visit my orphanage. When I was younger, I was afraid to go back because I thought they would leave me there—at least that's what my parents told me I said. As an adult, I felt very much at home. I definitely didn't feel like a tourist. I even made an effort to speak Spanish. I can safely say that while I was in Bogotá, I wasn't looking for my birth

*"When adoption set me apart from my family, whether innocently or maliciously, that's when it hurt."*

*"If you explain to people how your life situation came about,*
*the next time they come across a Hispanic Jew, they'll have a context for it."*

mother. I wasn't looking at every supermarket cashier, thinking, "Maybe she's my birth mother." Though if I found out a month from now that my parents could arrange for me to meet her, I definitely wouldn't shy away.

I identified with all the kids in the orphanage, and felt connnected to the place. It was a beautiful home, not the nightmarish image we have from stories. There was a little boy named Oscar. He was ten years old and we played soccer for hours. I had dreams of bringing him home with me—not to help him, but because he was terrific. But that wasn't possible. I don't picture myself as having been saved by my parents. I feel as grateful that my parents adopted me as they do. Some of our clients have definitely expressed the desire to help a child in Colombia or Guatemala, to bring that child to the United States to give him or her a "better life." It's interesting because you'd think that people who are infertile would just want to have a child, first and foremost. We try to steer them away from that language. Aside from the impact it has on the children —making them feel too indebted to you—when you're dealing with an orphanage in a foreign country or anyone in a foreign country, you don't want to offend them by suggesting that anything is wrong with growing up in that country.

I've experienced prejudice hundreds of times. It was easier to deal with when I was younger because my brother and sister were always there to protect me. As I got older, I was able to protect myself. I'm a little intolerant of the ignorance. One time I was pulled over by the police while driving my sister's BMW with my fiancée, Janice, who is Irish American. They asked her if she was okay, at which point she became enraged. Then they asked, "Whose car is this?" They never would have stopped me if I wasn't with a white girl. Luckily I was in law school at the time, and I knew I didn't have to tolerate this. I did end up getting a ticket—I didn't have my insurance card because it wasn't my car. I handled it well. I knew not to let the police officer get the better of me. I was most upset because all he could see was this Hispanic male driving with a white girl in a BMW, and that didn't seem right to him. His explanation was that I went around the curve too quickly. There actually was no reason for them to pull me over.

Sometimes I use these terrible situations as opportunities to help educate. My feeling is that if you explain how your life situation came about, the next time they come across a Hispanic Jew, they'll have a context for it.

**Janice:** When people ask, "Who are you marrying?" and I say, "James Greenberg," they assume that I'm marrying a Jewish guy. Then they see him, and they say, "Wait a minute, is he from Israel or something?" I tell them he's from Colombia. "I didn't know there were any Jews in Colombia," people remark. Then, generally, because ninety percent of the people keep asking me, I say, "He's adopted." And they say, "Oh really?" And then in a grave voice ask, "Does that bother you?" We get that a lot.

I feel a deep connection to Jaime because, though I wasn't exactly adopted, I was raised by my stepfather. My biological father held me, raised me—if you could call it that—for a year, and just walked away. Jaime, on the other hand, knew that his biological mother loved and cared about him, that she left him because she thought that was best for him. The questionnaire answered by his birth mother asked, "Why are you giving your child up for adoption?" And, in her own words, she replied, "I love my boy, I want him to have what I can't give him." I cried when I read that—crying for myself. Jaime was not rejected, nor does he feel rejected. But I was left by my father when I was already a year old. That feels like rejection. It also made me feel that maybe there was something wrong with me; that I deserved to be left. The tables are turned for us. Rather than my having to tell Jaime that there's nothing wrong with him, he's the one who has to tell me, "Your father's behavior has nothing to do with you, Janice." Luckily, my relationship with my stepfather is wonderful. I call him Dad. It's funny that Jaime would be the one to teach me, the child of a divorce, about the greater value of being adopted by someone who truly cares for you than being raised by a biological parent who cannot.

**Jaime:** When I think about having children, my first impulse is not to adopt. I probably will end up adopting, but not right off the bat. Janice and I definitely want to try to have biological children. I've never seen that biological connection to myself, and I'd like to. Our kids will be in big trouble. Just think about their background: Their mother will be a Jew, converted from Irish Catholicism. Their father is a Jew from Colombia. Their maternal grandfather will be Italian, and those aunts and uncles all Italian. Their paternal grandmother and grandfather will be Jews from Poland and Russia. They'll be so confused. And if they're adopted. . . . The gene pool will be interesting. It's going to be great, because the kids will be exposed to everything.

*"It's funny that Jaime would be the one to teach me, the child of a divorce, about the greater value of being adopted by someone who truly cares for you than being raised by a biological parent who cannot."*

# Philip

## "The fact is, I feel just as close to my adoptive parents as any kid who was raised by their biological parents."

Journalist and media marketing executive Philip Whitney, age thirty-six, was adopted domestically in a closed adoption at birth in 1963 by Ruth Whitney,* editor in chief of *Glamour* magazine, and the late Daniel Whitney, an advertising executive.

*Ruth Whitney died subsequent to this interview.

It may seem odd, but I've spent so little time in my life thinking about adoption. It's just not the way I identify myself. It's so matter-of-fact to me because my parents were always so open and direct about it. They first told me when I was very young—too young, in fact, to really know what it meant. I only remember that they made it clear that I was adopted, and that I was very special to them.

I do, however, remember one incident that resulted in my talking with my mother about being adopted. I was five or six years old and we were ice-skating together on a pond in the forest that abutted our house. I fell and hit my head on the ice very hard. (This sounds like a Stephen King novel where the kid falls through the ice and has a near-death experience.) It was probably almost a concussion. When I awoke I was woozy, and for some reason the first thing I started talking about to my mom was my adoption. I don't know why she chose that traumatic moment, but she then told me about a baby brother she'd given birth to after adopting me, and that the infant was premature and died after only a couple of hours of life. The whole discussion ended there.

The fact is, I feel just as close to my adoptive parents as any kid who was raised by their biological parents. Maybe more. Being biologically connected in my mind doesn't give you one up. Perhaps theoretically it should, but I don't feel that it does. What matters most is what's in your head.

I say that "theoretically" the biological component should matter because it would allow for some unspoken connection, a belief that since this child is of my genetic

material, there is some absolutely, irrefutable bond between us. But I don't believe that to be the case. I believe that so much of a parent-child relationship is based on nurturing. In the great debate over what matters more, nature versus nurture, I'm a strong believer that nurture is far more dominant a factor in child development.

I definitely feel that I am my parents' kid. I'm the exact midpoint between my mother and my father in terms of personality, predisposition, interests, and so on. My father was the director of his own advertising agency. He died in 1995. My mother was the editor in chief of *Glamour* magazine for many decades. My father was pretty scientific; he was a secular humanist. He was a very capable man; he took care of things. My mother, on the other hand, was very vulnerable, sensitive, and empathic. I feel I have qualities of both of them. In general, my interests were closer to my father's, but I ended up gravitating toward my mother's work.

Because I was such a scientific little kid, it was very easy for me to accept adoption as very normal. You get used to the fact that you're adopted, and the most important relationship in your young life is with your adoptive parents. It becomes a nonissue because of its banality. Graduating from high school, getting a date were more important to me. As I got older and learned about why people adopt or why people give children up for adoption, I understood why people did what they did. It seemed very logical to me. I never felt any resentment toward my birth parents for giving me up. My parents made it very clear when I was young that I

was a very special child because I was so wanted. The fact that they went out of their way to bring me into their lives has had a powerful effect on me.

Ironically, I grew up feeling sort of superior to other children. In those difficult times when children tease each other as they discover each other's weaknesses, kids tried to tease me about adoption. I would respond by saying, "Who are you kidding? You're the fourth child in a family and your parents barely even talk to you. My parents wanted me and love me, and I have a good life." Actually, because I was a fat kid, I was teased more often about being fat. Few kids knew that I was adopted, anyway. I felt lucky that I was adopted.

I had a kind of idyllic childhood. There was a forest near my house. I loved to just wander around or stare at and study the bark of a tree.

Not that I didn't have my share of problems. I developed an independent streak early on. I always believed that I'd have to be able to support myself; that I am the only person I can truly depend on. And that in a way has made me very self-confident. I'm not sure if my sense of independence is a result of being adopted or of being an only child. Both of my parents worked, and I was alone a fair amount of the time. I engaged in a lot of imaginative play on my own. I certainly remember that at a relatively early age I thought I was smarter than everybody else. That may have been true when I was a child just because I had so much more time to think than most kids. I didn't have as many people to interact with. I probably felt pain from being alone more than anything else.

But I never felt neglected or that my mother was too busy for me. I knew she would always be there. She took the 5:10 train home every night and she was home at 6:00. My read on that is that it's not necessarily important to have a parent at the house every day at 3:00. It's the reliability of a parent's being there that matters.

When I was a teenager, though, I did have an angry streak. And at a certain point I would argue with my parents and say, "Hey, you've done your job. I can take care of myself now, so stop trying to control me. Let go of the clamps." I got a bit rambunctious. I think that's possibly rooted in the fact that I was adopted. I thought, "Hey, I'm different from you; I'm separate and I can do anything I want." Then again, it may have been just another adolescent tactic.

In my early twenties, after I graduated from college, my mother asked me if I was interested in finding my biological parents. I think she was curious, but I wasn't. That's never really changed. The only time I was interested in my birth parents was when I was an adolescent. I wanted to know what I was going to look like. But that passed very quickly. It's logical that when you're searching to identify yourself that you'd want some kind of road map.

I'm not sure where I was adopted from. I've seen my birth certificate and there was an agency involved. After the adoption, the books were closed. I guess I feel that it would take a lot of work to look for my birth parents, and it's too much of a wild-goose chase for me. If I thought I was really going to discover something at the end of that search I might be more interested, but I feel like all I'll find at the end of the road will be old people. I'd ask, "Why did you give me up?" And they'd have one of a handful of reasons that I'd understand: We didn't have the money, we weren't married, or whatever. Other than that, I can't even imagine what I would talk to them about. Would they be that curious to know what I have been doing all my life and, if so, what does that do for me? I don't know what the trigger is that makes people pursue finding their biological parents. There are lots of other things I'm more curious about, like learning how to speak French. I guess I don't mind having that mystery in my life.

There is one question in my life related, perhaps, to my adoption, which I'm now pursuing in therapy. When my father died, I completely rationalized his death. I thought, well, everybody has to die. He was seventy. I basically buried the pain. What I've found is that the way I dealt with my father's death and with my mother's illness—she has ALS—was to shut down my emotions. But you can't selectively do that. My therapist says that it was precisely because my parents treated my adoption as such a nonissue that my feelings of loss were never expressed. We probably should have talked about it a little more. But, I don't know, it just never seemed like an issue. It all sounds way too complex; but I am listening to my therapist's ideas. I definitely think that the denial has taken its toll on me. It's good to feel the reality of pain in your life. It's part of the human condition.

# Mia

## "I think there's a lot more to being adopted than kids let on. There's this need to protect your parents."

Textile importer Mia Klein, age thirty-six, was adopted at ten days old in 1963, and her brother, Steven, age thirty-nine, was adopted at three weeks old in 1960. Both were adopted by Holocaust surivors in closed adoptions. Mia's birth mother found her when she was eighteen, but Mia didn't arrange for a meeting until thirteen years later.

My parents had a very tragic history. They were both Czech Holocaust survivors and had two biological children in Europe after the war. My mother and father were first cousins, and as a result, their son died at the age of ten and their daughter at four in America. They soon adopted a child, but eight months later the biological mother took the child back. Then they adopted me and my brother.

My mom would have given the world to see her children again. That's why, when my birth mom contacted me when I was eighteen, I think my mom understood her feelings about wanting to see me. She was incredibly generous to my birth mother in this regard, which is interesting, because generosity was totally out of character for both of my parents at the time. They weren't open or demonstrative people. They were completely shut down and numb. But they were open and supportive about that.

My mother wound up at Auschwitz at the age of eighteen. She watched her mother being killed, in front of her eyes. She saw her brothers and sisters destroyed. I really don't know the half of it because she wouldn't talk about it. I'm sure that the memories and the repression of all those feelings are what killed her. I never saw her cry. She was emotionally immobilized for years before she died. She was so damaged. I was extremely angry with her when I was a kid. I hated her. She started physically beating my brother and me when we were each around five years old. Today, they call that child abuse. To my mother this was discipline. I think that's how she had been raised: Break the spirit of the child and make the child obey.

While all this was happening, my father was doing the typical father thing—working day and night to make a comfortable life for his family. He became rich through real estate. He's an amazing man, but he didn't have a clue of how to be a father. He had no idea that my mother was beating us; my brother and I never

talked about it. We'd just see it happening to each other. I'd watch my brother hide in the curtains as my mother beat him, all the while shouting, "It doesn't hurt, it doesn't hurt." Talk about shutdown. On the other hand, I felt everything. I was very emotional. I ran away a few times, took drugs. I was never in therapy; I don't remember telling anyone about it. But I had a very strong spirit that couldn't be broken.

My parents were always very open about our adoption. It was probably the only thing about them that *was* open. "We chose you; we waited for you," my mother told me when I was three or four years old. I did have questions, but I never ever asked them. I don't know if there was a closed door, but it seemed to me that it would be difficult to talk about it.

I was always very curious about my genetic background. I'd look in the mirror and think, "Why do I look like this? My friends are so lucky; they look at their brothers and sisters and parents and they know who they look like." That was my most overriding anxiety. "You look like your mother," my aunt said to me. And I remember saying to her, "No, I don't. We all know what's going on here. Don't lie." Having true answers allows you to move on with your life.

I was fourteen years old the first time I remember hearing of this woman, my biological mother. Linda had decided that she should get in touch with my parents because she had given birth to a daughter who was severely hearing impaired, and her son also had a slight hearing deficit. She thought maybe she should contact my parents to let them know, just in case I had a problem that went undiagnosed. I remember my mother suddenly taking me for hearing tests. "Why are we doing this?" I asked my mother; then she told me the whole story about my birth mother contacting her. It was the first time I felt like there was this real physical person—this biological mother—out there. And then just four years later, I got the letter.

Linda had waited until I was of legal age to contact me. She, too, was adopted and had finally found her birth parents as well. She had always wanted to get to know me. When she was pregnant with me, she didn't want to give me up but was forced into it. Later, she raised three other children from different fathers. All her children always knew about me. They all celebrated my birthday every year. She and my biological father, Michael, went their separate ways after I was born. Michael went to university, became a lawyer, and never married. I'm his only child.

Linda's letter expressed all this love for me. I wrote back to her. She called me and we spoke on the phone. I was completely freaked out. She kept saying, "Oh, my daughter, my daughter." And I felt like, "Wait a minute. Wow. This is too much. You're not my mother, you're

*"Having true answers allows you to move on with your life."*

this woman I don't know." So we exchanged photos and letters. I wrote and said, "You know what, I'm not ready for this. I wanted to see what you looked like. But I'm kind of done for the moment."

Thirteen years later, at the age of thirty-one, I finally called Linda back. "I knew you would find me in your own time," she said. She came out and stayed with me for a week. It was an incredible meeting. Then she invited me out to meet the rest of the family. I couldn't help but notice the family resemblances in me.

Linda knew that I had also wanted to find my biological father. He was the love of her life, but it didn't work out. After some searching, I finally got him on the phone and we talked and talked, and in this very lawyerly fashion he said, "I suppose we should meet." I was going to wait a week, but two hours later he called me back and said, "Why not tomorrow?" So I went to see him the next day. We met for lunch and I stayed until midnight. Now we're the best of friends.

When Linda met my parents, they were very lovely to her. She thanked them and they each thanked her and they all said, "Look at the wonderful daughter we have." A year later, after my mother's death, my dad met Michael. Linda also got to see Michael again after thirty years! It's hard to put this all together. It's bewildering, but I feel very blessed.

For adopted children, that old question of nature versus nurture is very important. When I finally saw people in my biological family, I could sense the origins of some of my sensibilities. I feel like the person I am is more connected to my genetic history. Growing up, I thought, "I'm nothing like this family, nothing." But my parents had such a difficult, alien history, how could I feel otherwise?

I didn't really get to know my father until my mother passed away. After my mother died, he became a completely different person. When my mother was dying, he did everything for her, he went above and beyond. He's a hero, a whole book in himself. If it wasn't for him, his family would still be in Czechoslovakia. I've spoken to him about what my mother did to me and my brother. He didn't know and could only take in some of it. One year after my mother died, my father wanted to go back to Czechoslovakia. It had been fifty years. He, my brother, and I took this incredible journey into his past; it meant a lot to all of us. Now, I see him at least once a week and talk to him every day. I've gotten much of his story and we wrote it down together.

When I think about my mother now, given her history, how could she have been any different? But as a child, I didn't know about her suffering, and I couldn't forgive her. What she did to us wasn't forgivable. I forgive her now, finally.

After all of this, would I adopt? Absolutely.

I think there's a lot more to being adopted than kids let on. There's this need to protect your parents: They've taken care of you, gotten you through so many things. You don't want anyone to feel slighted or unappreciated. But, at the same time, you want to know about your history. When kids say they're not interested in knowing about their biological parents, it's only a partially truthful answer. I know because I was that way. It's tricky for everybody. For the parent, I can imagine loving your child so much that you would fear that this other person—this biological parent—will take away some of that love. I guess the best way to look at it is to acknowledge that your adopted kid wouldn't be around if it wasn't for the biological parents. You just have to come to terms with that.

In the final analysis, nobody will ever mean as much to an adopted child as the parents who raised her. No one, not even a biological family, can replace parents.

I never felt that my biological parents rejected me and that I was inferior to other kids. I suffered more because of how my mother treated me. As difficult as it was growing up with the parents I had, I feel fortunate. I could have wound up anywhere. And I absolutely believe that what I had to overcome I had to overcome. I'm a spiritual person and I believe that whatever we're given to deal with we're meant to be able to handle. When you're adopted, you begin at a very young age to ask the question, Why am I here? And it makes you—maybe—a little better at coming up with the answers.

*"Much of my anger went away after I met my birth mother. It made me more forgiving."*

# Sue

"Finding birth parents is a rebound, a reaction to what's normal in every child's development: the search for self."

Writer, producer, and film director Sue Wolf, age forty-two, was adopted domestically at four months in a closed adoption.

Being adopted was normal and wonderful for me; I always knew about it. I remember my parents reading me a book about adoption when I was very young. I loved that book, and I still remember its dark green cover and binding. It was *the* book. One night, I remember asking my mother, "Why? Why did they leave me?" And my mother said, "Because they wanted you to have a better life." And that seemed okay. I didn't really worry too much about it although I did have this fantasy that I had all these brothers and sisters.

My parents and I are very close. Symbiosis is an amazing thing, a nice mix of needs and desires. My dad is eighty and my mom is seventy-nine. My mother is Italian and fled Mussolini. My father is German and ran from Hitler. Neither of my parents is Jewish, though they both had Jewish relatives, and my father had a Jewish star stamped on his passport. They met on the boat on their way here. Both of them are very passionate, artistic, idealistic people. At some point with older parents, our attachment to them changes, and we become their caretakers. Since both my parents worked—they were teachers—they felt that one child was enough, so I'm the only one there for them.

On the whole, life was okay for me. It's funny, but often, when I was younger, people would say to me, "Oh, you look just like your father." He and I would wink at each other. It was cute, and I felt special as an adopted child. Still, on the issue of who I looked like, I was perplexed. I was always fascinated by that visible link. My

former husband has three brothers and a sister, and I was so excited to marry into a big family. To this day when I see people in a family who look alike, I stare at them forever! Adopted people have a need to know who they look like, to have a sense of the reality of their biological links. Ironically, I do have one friend who found her biological parents, and she doesn't look like them at all!

I don't think about biological connections or resemblances so much now, but I do think about the social and emotional issues raised by adoption for both birth and adoptive parents. It takes amazing strength for a mother to give up a child because she knows that her child's life will be better or just more livable. It's an honorable thing. I was angry about the "Baby Jessica" case. I felt both families were putting *their* needs before the child's.

Adoption can be a problem when kids become teenagers because of all the identity questions that naturally come up at that time. At sixteen, I'd say to my friends, "I can't stand my parents now. They won't give me the car. They don't know I smoke." But I'd always say, "I know they love me." I once screamed at my parents, "I'm going back to my real parents." I only said it once. It did hurt my parents, and I still feel bad about it.

However, I was never interested in looking for my birth parents. It might be that when you're a teenager and you're breaking away from your parents, you're more motivated to find birth parents, or even an estranged divorced parent. You might hope that it will answer many of the questions you're grappling with. But in the end, I think it's a false connection. It's a rebound, a reaction to what's normal in every child's development: the search for self. What worries me about searching for birth parents are the expectations one might have that one set of parents could replace another.

My adoptive aunt worked at the agency from which I was adopted. When I was in my twenties, she took me to lunch and told me things about my records. I didn't really want to know. She told me my dad was a famous baseball player and my mom was a secretary.

My parents were always open about my adoption. When I told my mom about my conversation with my aunt, she reminded me, "I have all of your papers in a safe-deposit box. You had another name. I have all the information if you want it, but you never asked for it." But I had simply never been interested in reading that information. However, when my parents moved, I did take the papers from their safe-deposit box and put them in mine, just in case I wanted to look at them on my own someday.

I'm thinking of adopting. I believe adoptive parents may possibly try harder to be good parents. Just about anybody can have a baby, but adopting takes a lot of courage. You have to go through the mill—you're grilled and you pay. Adoptive parents, by virtue of the process, are already primed like a pump to work at it. I think biological parents should have to get a license to have a kid, to take some classes and tests. You don't have to pass but just be exposed to the issues.

I had a delightful exchange with my parents when I spoke to them about wanting to adopt a Chinese baby girl. I was frustrated by all the agencies trying to get my business by telling me *they* would pick the very best baby for me. I wanted to go to China and choose my own child, I told my mother. She laughed and said, "Well, we didn't have our choice with you. We got a call and we went to look." My dad said, "All I did when I saw you was try to make sure you followed my finger with your eyes to check if you were alert." When I did, he said, "She's smart." My mom added, "Then you smiled at your dad and we said, 'Okay, we'll take her!'" So even though my parents say they didn't *exactly* choose me, I still got the "chosen child" story, the "you're special" story, which I believed then and believe now! It makes me happy.

I also spoke to my aunt about adopting a child. She implied that her agency would find it problematic that I never wanted to find my biological parents, and they would take that to mean that I wouldn't be open to connecting my own child with the birth family. I got a little upset. My aunt then suggested I write a letter to my biological parents. By urging me to contact my birth parents, not only was she trying to improve my chances of adopting, I think she was also trying to tell me that she knew, through her agency, that my birth parents wanted me to contact them. I'm not sure; but it felt like there was a hidden agenda, which made me a little nervous.

I told my parents about it. "I don't want to lie to an agency and tell them I want to find my birth parents in order for them to find me more suitable as an adoptive parent." So I called another agency, the Pearl S. Buck Foundation. I explained that I had been adopted, and wanted to adopt a baby myself. I also told them I had not contacted, nor was I interested in contacting, my birth parents. They were fine about that. They couldn't have been more open, "Oh how wonderful. You were adopted and you want to adopt." I thought, "Perhaps my aunt's concern with my contacting my biological parents is her own filter. I don't have to contact them in order to be a viable adoptive parent."

I am very interested in hearing about other adopted people who become adoptive parents. I wonder if the identification with each other as adoptees makes it special in some way. I wonder if we share certain predispositions. Every therapist I've ever seen was always convinced that whatever sadnesses and frailties I had were due to the trauma of adoption, of loss. I've never been convinced of that. Many of my friends, who were not adopted, have similar feelings. Can you really trace that to anything in particular? Being adopted is part of the recipe of who you are, but it's not the main ingredient.

I have a friend whose father didn't tell her she was adopted until he was drunk one night and it just came out of him. She was already twenty-five. She's never gotten over the betrayal of not being told earlier and in a loving way. Parents have to make it safe. That's all any child wants, to feel safe with their parents.

# Birth
# Mothers

Revealing the unexpected faces of love

# Daria

## "No one in my family expected the adoption to be as open as it has become."

Apprentice photographer Daria Stevens gave birth to Thomas in 1996, when she was twenty years old. He was adopted by Steve and Diana (interviewed on page 10) in an open adoption. Daria and birth father Damien have an active relationship with Thomas, age three, and his parents. Daria is now married to Ted Stevens and is the mother of Jacob, age four months.

It's amazing for me to see the difference between my two boys. Thomas, who was adopted by Steve and Diana, is very rambunctious and very lively. Yet Thomas's birth father, Damien, is very reserved. Thomas is actually quite the opposite of him. Ironically, Ted, my husband and Jacob's father, unlike my quiet little Jacob, is quite boisterous and outspoken. My sons are both pretty good examples that you cannot predict temperament by genetics alone.

Sometimes I think Thomas's boisterousness comes from my mood while I was pregnant with him. I was emotionally stressed—not so much because of Thomas, but because of the turmoil in my life. Damien and I had been together for about a year before I became pregnant. We broke up the day I got the pregnancy test results back. I hadn't told him right away, because I didn't want it to affect what was going on between us. I didn't want it to seem like I was trying to manipulate him.

At first, I had made an appointment to get an abortion and was told I had to wait four weeks. I knew I didn't really want to have one. I'm not against abortion, but in Thomas's case I just had this intuition that he was meant to be. When I told Damien I wanted to have the child, his response was basically, "It's your body. It's your decision," though he was uncomfortable with it. He supported me as much as he could, but it was a strain because we had pretty much decided that our relationship was over.

My mom's response was quite interesting. At first she said, "Okay, I'm going to be a grandmother." Several days later she said, "No, I think you should have an abortion." In the end, it didn't matter. I knew Thomas was meant to be born. I had this absolute knowledge that the path I was on was the right one. From the beginning, in my mind it was a fact that Thomas was going to be a boy, and I knew he was going to be born on a Wednesday—all of which turned out to be true. Things like that kept happening. I really gave myself over to my intuition, and trusted everything. After Thomas was born, I had a tattoo with his name and birthday in the shape of a necklace inscribed over my heart to symbolize my belief in the rightness of his existence.

When I discovered I was pregnant, the first thing I did was go to the phone book and call adoption centers. One agency informed me that I could choose the parents, and in the selection process I would get photographs and letters from the prospective parents; I would have medical expenses and living expenses covered for six months.

Damien helped me choose Thomas's parents. We met with three couples. The couple Damien connected with had just come out of fertility treatment and were still in mourning. They were filled with pain and emotional turmoil; I think their pain corresponded to what Damien was feeling. I thought Steve and Diana would make the best parents; I had a lot in common with them and felt there was good chemistry between us. One of the things that really impressed me about them

was that they knew what they wanted to do, and how they wanted to do it. They were the first people who immediately said, "We would like to meet you." They also presented me with a mass of information, whether it was in their favor or not.

It was Diana and Steve who were really into open adoption. They gave me Lois Melina's *The Open Adoption Experience*, which proved to be important to the whole process. No one in my family expected the adoption to be as open as it has become. We all anticipated having mixed feelings about it, and we worried that there would be a lot of pain when we went to see Thomas. But in the end, the more I got to know Steve and Diana, the less painful thoughts occurred to me. They were extremely supportive and have always respected our relationship. They are so much like family, after all.

Halfway through my pregnancy with Thomas, I moved down to Maryland. I spent my weekends with Steve and Diana. They became my birthing coaches and went to birthing classes with me. They were so present during my pregnancy that it was just as much their pregnancy as it was mine.

When Thomas was born, and I was to give him over to Steve and Diana, I decided that I wanted to mark the occasion in some public way. I got the idea to have an entrustment ceremony from one of the books on open adoption. I thought the ceremony would symbolize the transition from Thomas "belonging" to his birth parents to "belonging" to his adoptive parents. In many ways it parallels the ritual of the father of the bride "giving away" his daughter to a new family.

The ceremony was an overwhelming emotional experience, powerful beyond words. I cried the whole time. Without it, I wouldn't have had the opportunity to deal as fully with my emotions. It was a cathartic, healing process, and very good for me psychologically.

One of the most important benefits of the ceremony was that it brought my family together. They were there to see that we were giving Thomas to Steve and Diana, and he was not being taken away from anyone. Everybody in my extended family feels connected to him. Being together created a direct bond between them and Diana and Steve. The ceremony validated Thomas as still being a part of my family.

Whenever I come to visit Thomas, I get such a kick when he shouts, "Where's Daria, where's Daria?" I think I relate to him as an aunt. I'm still trying to invent an appropriate relationship. Diana explained to him that I'm the mommy in whose tummy he grew. It's awkward sometimes to express my feelings for him. I'm not sure how he'll take it, if he'll find it odd. The older he gets, the more assured I am that he feels comfortable with my caring so much about him, without my being there very often.

I see Thomas a couple of times a year for a few days. I have other family in the area, and I visit with them as well. Thomas is such a social guy. It's pretty hard not to relate to him on a direct level. He's so much fun to play with. I love how smart he is and how quickly he has developed. I love discovering all the things he's interested in. My mom has a direct relationship with him, but some people in my family worry about imposing on Steve and Diana. They don't realize how open the situation is.

Since Thomas was born, I've always said, "I am a mother, I have a kid." It's been strange sometimes, because in some situations people will see me with Jacob and ask, "Oh, is he your first?" And I'll say, "Well, yes." Then, at other times, I'll say, "No, I have a three-and-a-half-year-old." That's a strange thing to deal with. But then I think, "My God, there's no way in the world I would have been able to take care of both of them."

When I was pregnant with Thomas, there were a few people who said, "If you really love your child, you'll take care of him yourself, you'll keep him." And I thought, "Do they understand what they're saying?" That's one of the things Damien kept saying to me; his mother is a social worker and her business is moving kids from one foster home to another. She sees a lot of bad situations. I don't think they've experienced this kind of adoption, particularly an open adoption. I hope that seeing how everything has turned out for Thomas has given Damien more hope. I know he, too, visits Thomas.

Steve and Diana are two of the most well-functioning people I've ever met. I'm also so excited to hear that they are adopting another baby, and that Thomas will have a sibling. A good family is not all that common these days. But for us it's been almost the best of both worlds. I felt I was lucky enough to be able to do what I needed to do, and that I had support from family and friends, and from Steve and Diana. We have a unique relationship. I feel so lucky.

# Diane

"She wanted to know everything about me, and I wanted to know everything about her. We were like mother and daughter, but we were also something else: We were lost friends."

Artist Diane Churchill is the birth mother of Virginia, age thirty-seven. Virginia found Diane when she was twenty, and they have been close ever since. Diane has raised two daughters, Tasha, age twenty-six, and Karina, age twenty-two.

Last year, after reading a book about birth mothers and adoption called *May the Circle Be Unbroken* by Lynn Franklin, I went to a meeting with other mothers who had placed their babies for adoption. For the first time in my life I made contact with other women who had gone through what I had. I actually found myself feeling both envious of and glad for all the support that's offered to birth mothers today. I had none of that when I became pregnant in my senior year of college in 1962. I was completely alone because of both my own feelings and the cultural prejudices against "unwed mothers" at the time. I was a mess, and I didn't know how to help myself. I had cut myself off from my parents and all of my roots. I think I unconsciously went out and got pregnant to really distance myself from my past.

The day after graduation, I went to a home for unwed mothers where I would give birth and then place my child for adoption. It was one of the kinder places of this sort that I had found. They were very concerned with the children's welfare, as it should be. But they did little for the mothers, and I still feel angry about that. We were there for months, and nobody helped us. I felt we were used for our babies.

My whole focus as a pregnant mother was to find the right parents for my baby. I felt very strongly that it wouldn't be fair to try to raise a child in my personally messed-up situation. I desperately wanted my daughter to have a really solid family. The best thing about this home was that it allowed me to choose her family, for which I'm eternally grateful. It was very uncommon back then for a birth mother to decide where her child would go. It was really the only thing I could do for my baby.

After Virginia was born, I went to New York to go to art school. It was a completely new world for me in every way: I had just come from college, I had just given up a child, and I was trying to change my life completely. I really went downhill and seriously hit bottom. The first five or six years were horrible. I went into therapy, which was frowned upon at the time. Once we started working on my problems, my life started turning around, and it did so very quickly.

Later, in 1972, I got married and had two wonderful daughters. They have been the most important, beautiful, and healing forces in my life. It's almost a miracle that I even had them—before I married I discovered that I had carcinoma of the cervix. I was terrified and thought I would have to have a hysterectomy. It threw me back into the destructive thinking of my past: "I'm being punished, I'm cursed, I'm not going to be able to have another baby." All of my self-hatred came out, and I felt shame. But I got through that both emotionally and medically with no further problems, and I had my daughters Tasha and Karina [pictured here]. Tasha graduated from Vassar and works in international humanitarian relief. Karina is a student at St. John's College in Santa Fe. They're both marvelous human beings.

I didn't want it to be a family that just sounded good. I had this vague sense that I would know when I found the right one. I was presented, through their letters, with a number of potential adoptive families; what impressed me most about the parents was the voices that came through, not the information. When I read the letter from Virginia's mother, bells went off. I felt such joy and peace; I felt that I knew her. I think that my positive response also had a big impact on her later when we met. She knew that I had chosen her, and I think that helped lessen the inevitable feelings of competition between us.

Virginia and I finally met seventeen years ago, when she was twenty. She had wanted to find me for a long time, but she felt a particular urgency when she was a senior in college. Her parents, Margaret and Dick, were incredible, loving people, and they went out of their way to help her. They didn't have much to go on, and I've always felt badly about that. I could have signed up with one of the registries; that way I wouldn't have intruded on her life. I used to think, "When Virginia is fifteen, I'll make more of an effort to find her," and then I'd change the age. But each time, when the time came around, I was afraid. My life was fragile at times, and I had to hold my family together. I didn't know how much I could take. I had been searching, too, but I did it very timidly, and only sporadically.

Dick is a minister and is the coolest, loveliest, most intelligent man. He and Margaret had always known my name, and after a complicated series of searches they found me through an art dealer I had worked with.

On Christmas Day of 1982, they gave Virginia the information. It took her until Easter to write me a letter. When I received it, I was stunned—it was such an affirmation of life. It came at exactly the moment I needed it most because my marriage had been falling apart. Reading it was like uncovering an archaeological object that I'd been searching for my whole life. It was such a sensitive, intelligent, honest, and courageous letter that, reading it over and over again, I felt I knew so much about her. One of the things that so touched me was a purple heart sticker on the back of the envelope. I called Virginia afterward. I think the first thing I said to her was, "Purple is my favorite color."

And she said, "Oh, it's mine, too." That letter has never left my purse.

I don't know what happened after that. I was in a stupor. Somehow we made arrangements to meet within the next two weeks. I was just floating. No one knew, not even my kids. I was living this miracle, and I couldn't believe it.

Our first meeting was amazing. Virginia was a senior at the George Washington University. She came to New Jersey by train. I wore a Mexican dress; I knew that Mexico was a special place for her. I almost couldn't bear the wait at the station. Then I saw this beautiful girl. I wanted her to look like me, but I didn't think she did. She came up to me and we hugged and I looked into her eyes. It was an experience I can't describe. I felt weak. I think I felt as though I saw her whole life.

We spent the weekend together at my home, cooking, talking, looking, talking. It was magic. She was so lovely, so open. She wanted to know everything about me, and I wanted to know everything about her. We were like mother and daughter, but we were also something else: We were lost friends.

I think that in the intensity of the experience, I lost a sense of boundaries. At times I felt as if we were merging. We were constantly holding hands and touching. We couldn't be far away from each other for

*"Unlike the child who you raise, the child who you give up becomes a child of your imagination with whom you become preoccupied."*

long. I couldn't hold anything back. I assume this happens with other birth mothers who have had a happy reunion with their children. I must say I was awed by her. She is a fabulous, precious person.

The whole reunion experience was a bit like giving birth. You bond and fall in love. It's so physical and so intense. When you're raising a child, you go through many different periods together over the years. We went through all of that in a very compressed way. We even suffered the painful separation of adolescence—even though Virginia was older, she still needed to separate from me and all this intensity. She needed to work things out, which was healthy.

Margaret, Dick, and I met a month later, and we communicated often. They were very loving to me, and Margaret and I became very close. Sadly, Margaret died four years ago.

One of the challenges I faced after meeting Virginia was her reunion with my other two daughters. They were five and ten years old at the time; how could they picture their mother having given up a child? A close friend who was a therapist said a wonderful thing: She talked about bringing them into the joy. One night when my girls and I were watching a television show about an adopted child who found her birth mother, I realized that this was the right time to tell them they had a half sister and that they were going to be able to meet her. We had a family gathering in 1983 for my mother's seventieth birthday, and Virginia came to meet everyone.

Over the years I've seen that Virginia and I share certain mannerisms—small things, like ways of moving or laughing. Sometimes we even seem to look alike, though I don't think we do in reality. It's as though we had come out of the same pain. Unlike the child who you raise, the child who you give up becomes a child of your imagination with whom you become preoccupied. Virginia had written in her first letter something like, "I've thought about you every day of my life." And I could say the same thing. I'd like to think that it was because we were always loving each other that we were fortunate in our connection. I couldn't believe more that you heal in both body and soul when you're reunited. It's critical to have that connection resolved.

All kids, not just adopted kids, have issues to struggle with. Maybe that sounds like a bit of denial, but it's good for me to think that way because I carried all this fear and worry about Virginia and the circumstances of her life. She has told me about some of the pain she felt as an adopted child, despite how much she loved her parents. I can't help but be glad that she had such a good family. I felt I couldn't have given her what she needed at the time. I understand her feelings now. I used to have such a longing to make it lighter, easier. But I can no longer beat myself up or wring my hands. Life is an incredible mystery, and we have to work hard. I knew nothing about Virginia for twenty years. I think that if I had had contact with her, it would have saved both of us a good deal of suffering. I do wish I had raised my daughter. I wish she had been my baby and my little girl. I only feel bad that I didn't have the self-confidence to do it at the time.

# Acknowledgments

My gratitude to the families who opened their lives to me so that others may benefit from their experiences. I would like to thank the many individuals and families who spoke with me but whose stories, due to space constraints, could not be included in this book: Carolynne and Dan Butler, Ilene Meltzer, Wesley Brown, Rainah Berlowitz, Bill Barry, Mary Jane, Andrew, David, and Claudia Lewis, Cynthia McClintock, Kelly Meehan, Cheryl Beil, Judith Modell, Amy Strickler, Abby Ruder, Nancy Brett, Wayne Steinman, Sal, and their daughter Hope, Betsy Bartollet, Elaine Greene, Lisa Silverstein, Klara Silverstein, Casey Chamberlain, Laura Orsini, Peter Piatgorry, Marc Gross, Jan Heller Levy, Kacy Andrews, and Heather Degenhardt.

To the many organizations, therapists, and experts in adoption, thank you for sharing your wisdom and resources: Mary Sullivan and Amy Thurston of NAIC, the National Adoption Center, Lesbian and Gay Parenting, RESOLVE, the Open Door Society of Pennsylvania, the Adoptive Parents Committee of New York, Full Circle Adoptions, United Methodist Family Counselling, Holly McGuiness of AKA, Sandy Ripburger and Nancy Wallen of Spence-Chapin, Claire Timmony and Joe Kelly of Families with Children from China (New York City Chapter),

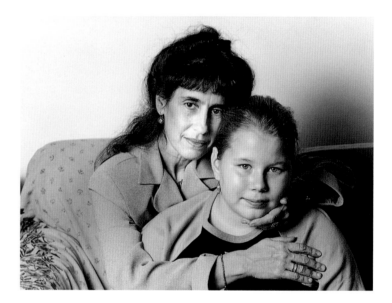

Arthur D. Sorosky, M.D., Arlene Stang, Phyllis Lowenger, Joyce Pavao, Adam Pertman, and Lynn Franklin.

To my family and friends who have given me so much support and encouragement over the two years that I have dreamed of and worked on this project: my brother and sister-in-law, Mark and Hannah Kinn, the parents of my beloved niece, Sarah; and my father, Philip Kinn. My friends: Eric Lindbloom and Nancy Willard, Judith Raphael, Tony Phillips, Jim Jubak, Ellen Kozak, Susan Ochshorn, Janice Vallely, Morris Eagle, Ronni Stolzenberg, Ralph Sassone, Myra Goldberg, Lucy Rosenthal, Kathleen Hill, Flavio Perpetuo, Esther Cohen, Lynne Meehan, Francis Rudnick Levin, M.D., Ilja Wachs, Maryanne Burke, Deborah Tanklow, Marie D'Amico, Elizabeth Benedict, and Susan Price.

To my agent, Susan Ginsburg, of Writer's House, who believed in this book.

To the people and friends at Artisan who provided vision, expertise, and heartfelt support for this project: Dania Davey for her lovely design, Nancy Murray for producing this against all odds, Tricia Boczkowski for her thoughtfulness. Thanks to publicity director Liz Hermann. And special thanks to Deborah Weiss Geline, for her professionalism, grace, and understanding. To Laurie Orseck for her insightful and very fine, fine-tuning of the manuscript. Finally, to my editor and publisher, Ann Bramson, for her steadfast belief in this book, her gift for making beautiful books happen—and for her friendship.

And to Ken Shung, my photographer, for his brilliant work. How lucky I found you.

—*Gail Kinn*

First, I am deeply grateful to the people and the families who let me share their time in the making of these portraits. I am most thankful to Gail Kinn for believing in me and sharing the vision of this project. I must also thank Patti Ratchford for her recommendation, and the following for their support and workmanship throughout the years: Eddie Skuller, Katharine Pollak, and David Wong and his staff. Thanks also to my longtime friends Kevin and Eugene Moore, who always appreciated the camera that I would carry with me from the beginning. Finally, I am forever beholden to my wife, Jung Hyang, and daughter, Taylor Ava, for making my life one of love and understanding.

—*Ken Shung*

# Resources

Bolles, Edmund Blair. *The Penguin Adoption Handbook.* New York: Penguin Books, 1993.

Brodzinsky, David M., Ph.D.; Marshall D. Schechter, M.D.; and Robin Marantz Henig. *Being Adopted: The Lifelong Search for Self.* New York: Anchor Books/Doubleday, 1993.

Caplan, Lincoln. *Open Adoption.* New York: Farrar, Straus & Giroux, 1990.

Fraiberg, Sylvia H. *The Magic Years.* New York: Charles Scribner, 1959.

Franklin, L. C., with E. Ferber. *May the Circle Be Unbroken.* New York: Harmony Books, 1998.

Gasco, Elyse. *Can You Wave Goodbye, Baby?* New York: Picador, 1999.

Gilman, Lois. *The Adoption Resource Book,* rev. ed. New York: HarperCollins, 1992.

Howard, Jane. *Families.* New York: Simon & Schuster, 1978.

Lifton, Betty Jean. *Journey of the Adopted Self: A Quest for Wholeness.* New York: Basic Books, 1994.

Melina, Lois Ruskai. *Raising Adopted Children.* New York: HarperCollins, 1998.

———. *Making Sense of Adoption: A Parent's Guide.* New York: Harper & Row, 1989.

———. *The Open Adoption Experience.* New York: Harper & Row, 1993.

Mitchard, Jacquelyn. *The Rest of Us: Dispatches from the Mother Ship.* New York: Viking Penguin, 1997.

Pavao, Joyce Maguire. *The Family of Adoption.* Boston: Beacon Press, 1998.

Rosenberg, Elinor B. *The Adoption Life Cycle.* The Free Press, 1992.

Saffian, Sarah. *Ithaka: A Daughter's Memoir of Being Found.* New York: Basic Books, 1998.

Schaeffer, Carol. *The Other Mother: A True Story.* New York: Soho Press, Inc., 1991.

Schaeffer, Judith, and Christina Lindstrom. *How to Raise an Adopted Child.* New York: Crown Publishers, 1989.

Sorosky, Arthur D., M.D.; Annette Baran, M.S.W.; and Reuben Pannor, M.S.W. *The Adoption Triangle: Sealed or Open Records: How They Affect Adoptees, Birth Parents, and Adoptive Parents.* New York: Anchor Press/Doubleday, 1978.

Wadia-Ells, Susan, ed. *The Adoption Reader: Birth Mothers, Adoptive Mothers, and Adopted Daughters Tell Their Stories.* Seattle: Seal Press, 1995.

Watkins, Mary, and Susan Fisher. *Talking to Young Children About Adoption.* New Haven: Yale University Press, 1993.

Wolff, Jana. *Secret Thoughts of an Adoptive Mother.* Kansas City: Andrews and McMeel, 1997.

**CHILDREN'S BOOKS**

Curtis, Jamie Lee, and Laura Cornell, illustrator. *Tell Me Again About the Night I Was Born.* New York: HarperCollins, 1996.

Kasza, Keiko. *A Mother for Choco.* New York: Putnam, 1992.

Krementz, Jill. *How It Feels to Be Adopted.* New York: Alfred A. Knopf, 1982.

## NATIONAL ADOPTION ORGANIZATIONS

National Adoption Information Clearinghouse
P.O. Box 1182
Washington, D.C. 20013-1182
web site: http://www. naic@/calib.com
202-842-1919

Adoptive Parents Committee
(listings in New York, New Jersey,
Pennsylvania)
212-304-8479 (New York chapter)

Adopted Families of America
2309 Como Avenue
St. Paul, Minnesota 55108
651-645-9955

Child Welfare League of America
440 First Street N.W.
Third Floor
Washington, D.C. 20001-2085
202-638-2952
web site: http://www.cwla.org

Open Door Society (listed by state)
1-800-93-ADOPT
web site: http://www.odsma.org

Council on Adoptable Children
(listed by state)
National Adoption Center
1-800-TO-ADOPT

RESOLVE (listed by state)
212-410-2270 (New York chapter)

Spence-Chapin Services to Families
and Children
212-369-0300 (New York chapter)

New York State Citizen's Coalition
for Children
607-272-0034
web site: http://www.nysccc.org

## INTERNATIONAL ADOPTIONS

Joint Council on International
Children's Services
301-322-1906
web site: http://www.jcics.org

International Concerns Committee
for Children
911 Cypress Drive
Boulder, Colorado 80303
303-494-8333

Also Known As, Inc.
212-386-9201 (New York chapter)
web site: http://www.akaworld.org
E-mail: alsoknownas@onelist.com

Association of Korean Adoptees
(Los Angeles and San Diego chapters)
Box 87291
San Diego, California 92138
E-mail: akasocal@geocities.com
415-339-7447 (San Francisco chapter)

Families with Children from China
(listed by state)
212-579-0115 (New York chapter)

Latin American Adoptive Parents Association
LAPIS (listed by state)
201-438-9214 (New Jersey chapter)

## ADOPTION ATTORNEYS

American Academy of Adoption Attorneys
P.O. Box 33053
Washington, D.C. 20033-0053
202-832-2222

## CATALOG

Tapestry Books
P.O. Box 359
Ringoes, New Jersey 8551-0359
1-800-765-2367

## ADOPTION MAGAZINES

*Roots and Wings*
P.O. Box 638
Chester, New Jersey 07930
908-637-8828

*Chosen Child*
246 South Cleveland Avenue
Loveland, Colorado 80537
970-663-1185

*Adoptive Families*
2309 Como Avenue
St. Paul, Minnesota 55108
651-645-9955

## ADOPTION INTERNET SITES

http://adoption.com
http://www.adoptiononline.com
http://www.iwe.com/apact.html
http://www.adopting.org
http://www.rainbowkids.com
http://www.odsma.org